KT-454-067

Contents

Patrick Marber   v

Plot   x

Commentary   xiii
    Background and influences   xiii
    Structure and time   xxiv
    Identity   xxxii
    Sex and love   xlii
    Death   xlix
    Chance   liii
    London   lv
    Minor characters   lix
    Closer on stage   lxi
    Closer on screen   lxxiii
    Further viewing   lxxxiv

Textual Notation   lxxxix

Further Reading and Viewing   xci

CLOSER   1
    Appendix to Scene Three   116

Notes   121

Questions for Further Study   124

Unless otherwise indicated, all direct quotations from Patrick Marber in this Commentary are taken from my interviews with him in London in July and September 2005 and June 2006.

References to and quotations from 'the NT Studio draft' of *Closer* refer to the script that was given a rehearsed reading at the National Theatre Studio on 13 December 1996, and are cited by kind permission of the author.

I would like to thank Georgina Allen, my editor, Gavin Clarke (National Theatre Archive) and, especially, Patrick Marber for their invaluable help in the preparation of this edition.

D.R.

Patrick Marber

1964   Born in London on 19 September 1964.

1975– Attends Rokeby Preparatory School, Kingston-
82   upon-Thames, then St Paul's School, London, and
        Cranleigh School, Surrey. At Cranleigh he plays the
        Fool in *King Lear* and the tramp, Davies, in Harold
        Pinter's *The Caretaker*.

1983– Reads English at Wadham College, Oxford.
86

1985– Appears with Guy Browning at the Edinburgh
87   Festival Fringe in a comedy double-act, *Dross Bros*.

1988– Performs on London cabaret circuit and tours
90   England as a stand-up comedian, with television
        appearances on *Friday Night Live*, *Nothing Like a Royal
        Show!* and *Paramount City*. Performs on Edinburgh
        Fringe as stand-up in shows with Jack Dee and Jo
        Brand.

1992   Co-writes and acts in spoof news comedy series *On
        the Hour*, broadcast on BBC Radio 4. At the
        Edinburgh Fringe directs Steve Coogan and John
        Thomson in a two-man show, *Steve Coogan and John
        Thomson in Character*, which wins Perrier Award for
        Comedy and transfers to London.

1993   In November, begins developing *Dealer's Choice* at
        the National Theatre Studio through a series of
        rehearsed readings and improvisations, culminating
        in a small-scale production in February 1994.

1994   Co-writes (with Steve Coogan and Henry Normal)
        and appears in *The Paul Calf Video Diary*, screened on
        BBC2 on 1 January. Co-writes and acts in six-part
        series *The Day Today*, a television spin-off from *On the
        Hour*, screened weekly on BBC2 in January and
        February. Appears in and co-writes (with Steve
        Coogan and Armando Ianucci) six half-hour

episodes of spoof chat show *Knowing Me, Knowing You . . . with Alan Partridge*, screened on BBC2 in September and October. Co-writes (with Steve Coogan and Henry Normal) *Three Fights, Two Weddings and a Funeral: Pauline Calf's Wedding Video*, and plays Spiros, Pauline's fiancé.

1995 Directs *Dealer's Choice*, opening performance on 9 February at the Cottesloe Theatre, London. The play transfers to the Vaudeville Theatre in May, where it runs until 28 October, and goes on to win the *Evening Standard* Award for Best Comedy and the Writers' Guild Award for Best West End Play. An international tour is mounted in 1996. Works on two episodes of the series *Coogan's Run* on BBC2, directing and co-writing *The Curator*, and co-writing and appearing as a quiz fanatic alongside Steve Coogan in *Natural Born Quizzers*. Writes and directs *After Miss Julie* for BBC2, first broadcast on 4 November, starring Phil Daniels (John), Geraldine Somerville (Miss Julie) and Kathy Burke (Christine). Co-writes and appears in *Knowing Me, Knowing Yule . . . with Alan Partridge*, a Christmas edition of the spoof chat show, screened on BBC2 on 29 December.

1996 Directs *'1953'* by Craig Raine, at the Almeida Theatre, London, opening performance on 14 February. Directs *Blue Remembered Hills* by Dennis Potter at the Lyttelton Theatre, London, opening performance on 2 May. Directs an international tour of *Dealer's Choice*, including participation in Cultural Olympiad at Atlanta Olympic Games. In September, spends a week at the National Theatre Studio on work-in-progress scenes for his second play, which will become *Closer*, with Douglas Hodge, Jason Isaacs, Anna Chancellor and Claire Skinner. In November, travels to Ireland and writes a full-length draft of the play in County Monaghan. In December, spends two weeks at the National Theatre Studio working on draft script of the play,

with actors Kate Beckinsale, Stephen Dillane, Sally
Dexter and Mark Strong.

1997   Directs premiere of *Closer* at the Cottesloe Theatre,
with Liza Walker (Alice), Clive Owen (Dan), Ciaran
Hinds (Larry), Sally Dexter (Anna), opening
performance on 22 May. The play transfers with
two new cast members to the Lyttelton Theatre on
16 October. It wins the Laurence Olivier Award,
the Critics' Circle Award and *Time Out* Award for
Best New Play and *Evening Standard* Award for Best
Comedy.

1998   On 19 March, *Closer* transfers to the Lyric Theatre,
Shaftesbury Avenue, where it runs until 31 October.
Directs *The Old Neighborhood*, three one-act plays by
David Mamet at the Royal Court (Duke of York's
Theatre), London, opening performance on 17
June, featuring Zoë Wanamaker and Colin Stinton
(Stinton speaks the last line in the film of *Closer*.)

1999   Directs *Closer* on Broadway at the Music Box
Theatre, opening on 25 March, starring Rupert
Graves (Dan), Ciaran Hinds (Larry), Anna Friel
(Alice) and Natasha Richardson (Anna). It is
nominated for Best New Play at the Tony Awards
and wins the New York Critics' Circle Award for
Best Foreign Play. Revival of *Closer*, directed by
Paddy Cunneen, opens at the Lyttelton Theatre on
20 December. Writes screenplay of *Asylum*, from the
novel by Patrick McGrath.

2000   Appears as the Hollywood movie executive Charlie
Fox in David Mamet's *Speed-the-Plow*, directed by
Peter Gill at the New Ambassadors Theatre,
London, and co-starring Mark Strong and Kimberly
Williams. Writes third play, *Howard Katz*. In
November, directs *The Caretaker* by Harold Pinter at
the Comedy Theatre, London, starring Michael
Gambon, Douglas Hodge and Rupert Graves.

2001   Directs *Howard Katz*, starring Ron Cook in the title
role; opening performance at the Cottesloe Theatre
on 13 June. Writes unproduced screenplay, *About the*

Author, based on the novel by John Colapinto, for
DreamWorks.

2002   Writes short film *The Egg*, directed by Richard
Wilson, starring Tim Healy, Jamie Beddard and
Frances de la Tour, broadcast on BBC2 on 2
October as part of the *What's Your Problem?* series.

2003   Writes screen adaptation of *Closer*. Stage premiere of
After Miss Julie at the Donmar Warehouse, London,
on 20 November, directed by Michael Grandage,
starring Richard Coyle (John), Kelly Reilly (Miss
Julie) and Helen Baxendale (Christine).

2004   Writes a short film, *Old Street*, for Channel Four,
directed by Angus Jackson, starring Ray Winstone,
David Tennant and Victor Romero Evans. Writes
The Musicians, a play for teenage actors, premiered at
the Olivier Theatre in July as part of the Shell
Connections project. The play follows the Ridley
Road School Orchestra to the European Festival of
Youth in Moscow, where their instruments are
impounded just hours before they are due to
perform Tchaikovsky's Fourth Symphony. Writes
radio play *Hoop Lane*, transmitted on BBC Radio 3
in November, starring Warren Mitchell and
Maureen Lipman. The film of *Closer* is released in
the US on 3 December, and in the UK on 14
January 2005.

2005   At the Golden Globe Awards in January *Closer* is
nominated for Best Motion Picture (Drama),
Marber is nominated for Best Screenplay and Mike
Nichols for Best Director, while Clive Owen wins
Best Supporting Actor and Natalie Portman wins
Best Supporting Actress. The National Board of
Review gives the cast its award for Best Acting by an
Ensemble. Owen and Portman are also nominated
in the supporting categories at the Oscars and the
BAFTA Film Awards, and Owen wins the BAFTA;
Marber is nominated for Best Adapted Screenplay.
Asylum, directed by David Mackenzie, competes at
the Berlin International Film Festival in February,

starring Ian McKellen and Natasha Richardson.
Writes screenplay for the film *Notes on a Scandal*
(directed by Richard Eyre), from the novel by Zoë
Heller, starring Judi Dench and Cate Blanchett.

2006   Writes *Don Juan in Soho*, a free version of Molière's
Don Juan, scheduled to open at the Donmar
Warehouse, London, on 30 November.

Plot

London, the 1990s.

Act One
Scene One: Dan, a thirty-five-year-old newspaper obituary
writer, has taken Alice, twenty-four, to hospital after seeing
her knocked down and slightly injured by a taxi. While she
waits for treatment he tells her about his work. Larry, a
dermatologist, walks past. He examines Alice because she's
a pretty girl, though she's not his responsibility. Dan and
Alice chat. Alice tells Dan she's been working as a stripper.
Dan tells Alice he has a girlfriend, Ruth. Alice persuades
Dan to call in sick and spend the day with her.

Scene Two: June, the following year. Dan and Alice are living
together. Anna, a photographer recently separated from her
husband, is taking Dan's portrait for the jacket of his
forthcoming first novel, which is based largely on Alice's life.
Instantly attracted, Anna and Dan kiss, just before Alice,
now working as a café waitress, arrives. Alice overhears Dan
demanding to see Anna again. She asks to have her picture
taken and when Dan has left, confronts Anna with what
she's heard.

Scene Three: January. At his computer, on an evening shift at
the hospital, Larry enters an internet chatroom and has
cybersex with Dan, who is pretending to be a woman called
Anna. Their virtual encounter ends with Dan inviting Larry
to meet 'Anna' the following day at the London Zoo
Aquarium and then have sex at a hotel.

Scene Four: Larry arrives at the Aquarium and, by chance,
meets the real Anna, who is celebrating her birthday alone.

She realises what has happened and explains that Dan has sent Larry on a fool's errand.

Scene Five: Five months later, Dan and Alice attend the private view for Anna's exhibition of photographs, which includes the picture of Alice taken at Anna's studio. Anna and Larry are now living together. Dan rejects Alice's suggestion that he is trying to leave her and insists that he loves her. Alice chats to Larry and reminds him where they've met before. Dan tells Anna he loves her and tries to persuade her to come away with him on a weekend trip to attend his father's funeral. She resists him but it later turns out that they are about to begin an affair.

Scene Six: Two intercut scenes on the same night, a year later. Dan tells Alice about his affair with Anna. Larry and Anna have married. Larry returns to their apartment from a medical conference in New York. Alice runs out on Dan. Larry confesses to having had sex with a New York prostitute. Anna confesses that she and Dan have been lovers since the private view and says she is leaving Larry.

Act Two

Scene Seven: Three months later, Larry visits a lapdancing club, where Alice is working. He pays her for a private striptease and tries to get her to admit who she is. He wants her to go home with him. She resists, or so it seems.

Scene Eight: The following month. Dan and Anna meet in a restaurant. Anna has just met Larry to sign their divorce papers, and the scene between them is shown in flashback: Larry blackmails her into having sex with him one last time before he signs. Anna tells Dan what happened.

Scene Nine: One month later, Alice has arranged to meet Larry at a museum. She gives him a birthday gift and exits. She has also arranged to meet Anna there, thus setting up a meeting with Larry. Anna is shocked when Larry tells her he's been sleeping with Alice since the night before they met to sign their divorce papers. Larry leaves Anna and Alice to compare their relationships with Dan and Larry. Alice still loves Dan and wants Anna to take Larry back.

Scene Ten: A month later. Larry and Anna are back together. In his surgery, Larry tells Dan to give up attempting to win Anna back and reveals where he can find Alice – and that he has had an affair with her.

Scene Eleven: A month later, in an airport hotel bedroom prior to going on holiday to New York to celebrate their fourth anniversary, Dan and Alice recall the details of their first meeting. When Dan tries to force her to confess to having slept with Larry she declares that she no longer loves him and is leaving. Dan hits her.

Scene Twelve: Six months later. In Postman's Park, Anna, single again, meets Larry, who is now seeing a young nurse, Polly. Dan has told them by telephone that Alice was knocked down and killed in New York the previous evening. Larry tells Anna that Alice had taken the name Alice Ayres from one of the park memorials, commemorating a woman who died saving three children from a burning house. Larry goes back to work as Dan enters. Dan tells Anna that Alice's real name was Jane Jones and also mentions that Ruth, his ex-girlfriend, has married and started a family. Dan leaves to catch a flight to New York to identify Alice's body.

Commentary

Background and influences

> It's generally true that there isn't a single seed of an idea.
> There are always lots of things going into the mix. (Patrick
> Marber)

In 1992, Patrick Marber was established as a successful
stand-up comedian and a writer-performer for the
acclaimed BBC Radio news spoof, *On the Hour*. At that
year's Edinburgh Festival, he directed the show featuring his
On the Hour colleague Steve Coogan, with John Thomson,
which won the prestigious Perrier Award for Comedy and
then transferred to London. Around this time, Marber's
then agent, John Wood, had been urging him to think about
writing for the stage. Wood invited Sue Higginson, head of
the National Theatre Studio, one of whose principal aims is
to develop new works, to see the Coogan show. 'After Sue
came, I had a meeting with her and she said, "Any ideas for
plays?"' Marber recalls. 'I said I was sort of interested in
doing a play about a poker game and she gave me a two-
week workshop at the Studio, which ultimately became my
first play, *Dealer's Choice*.'

Dealer's Choice was a major success at the National
Theatre's Cottesloe auditorium, winning the *Evening Standard*
Award for Best Comedy and the Writers' Guild Award for
Best West End Play. Set on one night, before, during and
after a poker game in a restaurant, it unfolds in a
testosterone-fuelled, blokeish environment in which *Closer*'s
Larry would probably feel at home and Dan would feel
uncomfortable. The play explores with great humour and
verve male power relationships: between father and son,
boss and employee, gamblers and their opponents. As an aid
in studying *Closer*, however, *Dealer's Choice* is much less
illuminating than the two pieces of work that followed it, not

least because they both contain complex and strong-willed female characters, and after the all-male *Dealer's Choice*, Marber 'was determined that my second play should have women in it'.

'1953'

In February 1995, Marber directed Craig Raine's verse drama *'1953'*, a version of Racine's *Andromaque* (first staged in 1667), at the Almeida Theatre in Islington, north London. Raine's reworking of the Greek myth transposes Racine's drama from the aftermath of the Trojan War to the year of the title and imagines that Hitler and Mussolini have won the Second World War, devastating England and destroying the British Empire. Orestes, an envoy from Hitler, arrives in Rome to demand from Vittorio Mussolini, son of Benito, the release to the Reich of his young English prisoner, Angus LeSkye, whom Hitler believes to be a danger to German interests. If Vittorio refuses, Germany will invade Italy. To strengthen the Axis, Orestes is also attempting to convince Vittorio to marry the German princess, Ira, with whom Orestes has had a passionate affair. But Vittorio is hopelessly in love with Angus's mother, the aristocratic Englishwoman, Annette. As in so much classical tragedy, the fate of nations hinges on individual desires, and the crisscrossing political agendas and sexual passions lead ultimately to Orestes murdering Vittorio and Ira killing herself.

As outlined here, the plot and setting may appear to have little in common with the modern London of *Closer*, but if you read *'1953'* after Marber's play, you sense immediately how he was influenced by immersing himself in Raine's script for weeks of rehearsal and performance. *Closer* echoes the rhythms and raw imagery of Raine's verse as it explores the selfishness of desire, especially at the many points when the four principal characters (two men and two women in both plays) reveal brutal truths to a prospective, current or former lover.

The brutish Vittorio has a touch of *Closer*'s Larry. Both

are macho 'cavemen' who fall for women of superior class and slip into foul-mouthed fury when rejected or betrayed: Vittorio calls Anne 'a patronising cunt' (*'1953'*, p. 20); Larry dismisses Anna with 'Now fuck off and die. You fucked-up slag' (p. 61). Certain speeches in *'1953'* could serve as commentary on the characters' actions and self-justification in *Closer*. Here, for example, is Orestes' response when Ira tries to wriggle out of eloping with him to Germany:

Orestes
> Ah-ha, passion's brilliant special pleading.
> The best-equipped Swiss army knife
> isn't more versatile, resourceful, ingenious. (p.34)

'Passion's brilliant special pleading' is a wonderful description for Anna's and Dan's explanations of why their illicit affair feels different from the day-to-day contact of life with, respectively, Larry and Alice. It's easy to imagine several more of Orestes' lines being applauded – or even quoted – by Dan. 'If Life is punishment, let's commit a crime' (p. 46), he says, anticipating the 'we're all going to die, so let's fuck' philosophy that Dan uses at the art gallery to convince Anna to sleep with him. Later, Orestes implores Ira to stop evading the truth about human motivation, namely that 'Love is selfish' (p. 49); Dan tells Alice he's leaving her for Anna 'Because . . . I'm selfish and I'll be happier with her' (p. 54). Moments such as these illustrate how in both plays the talk of passion and desire is cold and competitive; Raine's principal characters are all, like Larry, 'clinical observers of the human carnival'.

Although there are four subsidiary characters in *'1953'* (advisers, servants or friends of the principals), the most intense moments are provided by the one-on-one exchanges between two men, two women and, in particular, a man and a woman, which together make up at least half of Raine's play. The same applies to *Closer*, which is utterly dominated by the duologues between Alice and Dan, Anna and Dan, Larry and Anna, Larry and Alice. The tone, language and, above all, structure of Raine's play clearly fed into *Closer*.

'When I directed Craig's play, I perceived the shape of it very profoundly,' Marber explains. 'It's not a four-hander but the centre of it is two men and two women who all love each other in various combinations – so I was given the shape of *Closer*, really, for free by Craig's play.'

'After Miss Julie'

In 1995, the producer Simon Curtis approached Marber to adapt and direct August Strindberg's *Miss Julie* (1888) for Performance, the BBC2 strand for classical drama. 'Simon and the script editor Michael Hastings said "Be as free with it as you want",' says Marber. 'I think that seeing what Craig had done to Racine in *"1953"* inspired me to be radical with *Miss Julie*.'

In Marber's adaptation, John, a valet/chauffeur at a country estate, is engaged to the cook, Christine. He seduces the willing Julie, daughter of the lord of the manor, who has recently been jilted by her military fiancé. The following morning they prepare to elope to open a nightclub in New York, with a large sum of cash that Julie steals from her father. But when John refuses to let her take her pet bird with her and beheads it, she loses control. His Lordship suddenly summons John, whose rebellion evaporates instantly; he's once again as servile as ever. Overwhelmed by shame and hatred of men, Julie implores him to order her to kill herself. He gives her his razor and she goes out to slit her throat.

Marber made no significant changes to Strindberg's plot but changed names (the original has Jean, Kristin and Julie), locations and period to give an intriguing and distinctly English flavour to the gulf in social class and power struggle between servant and mistress. He moves us from late nineteenth-century Sweden to England on 26 July 1945, the night of the General Election, won in a landslide by Labour, who introduced a radical programme of nationalisation and new social services for all: the welfare state. Marber symbolically contrasts national upheaval with the intimate action of the play: on the night that the political party for whom the interests of the working-classes were paramount defeats the coalition government led by the Conservative Winston Churchill (himself the son of a lord), a servant 'triumphs' over the daughter of a lord. Julie is destroyed, but John is doomed to languish in the lowly position in which we first find him. 'Both of them lose,' says Marber, 'so what *After Miss Julie* is saying is that political change is more rapid than social change.'

Though the social metaphor in *Closer* is less pronounced, Marber acknowledges that Larry and Anna's relationship echoes John and Julie's; crudely put, both see well-bred women attracted by a lower-class 'bit of rough'. As with *'1953'*, there are revealing comparisons to be made between the sexually charged male–female encounters in *After Miss Julie* and *Closer*, and the plays' complementary attitudes towards love and sex. To take two early examples, the sustained mood of flirtatious curiosity as Julie questions John about his experience of the Second World War and of working for her father (*Plays: 1*, pp. 137–45) is, though pitched in a more ominous key, similar to the atmosphere of *Closer*, Scene One, as Alice and Dan question one another (indeed, although they have lived in the same house for years, Julie and John are as much strangers to one another as Alice and Dan). 'I daresay that there's a touch of Miss Julie in Alice,' suggests Marber. 'Julie is a carnal creature and knows it, and is both shockingly confident and insecure simultaneously.'

Earlier in *After Miss Julie*, the tension between John, Christine and Julie, and then between Christine and Julie on their own (pp. 134–6), resembles the latter part of Scene Two in *Closer*. In the aftermath of Julie and John's dance together, Christine senses her hold over her lover being threatened by another woman; Alice knows from eavesdropping that she is similarly threatened.

'What the Strindberg taught me,' explains Marber, 'is that if you start [a play] with a charged situation it's very good news. The charge at the beginning of *Miss Julie* is that this guy [Jean] is supposed to marry this woman [Kristin] and he's just had a dance with the other woman [Julie] and

Julie already knows that she kind of wants him, so before the play begins it's all happening.' By the end of the second scene in *Closer*, 'it's all happening' in that Dan and Alice's stability as a couple is being threatened by the other woman, Anna; although this time it is the older woman who'll become the 'thief' of the younger partner.

After Julie and John's night in bed, he warns her that she is foolish to 'confuse love with desire', evoking the conflict between enduring love and fleeting passion that is central to *Closer*. With dizzying speed, John's ardour turns to cruelty, a trait that he shares with Larry:

> **Julie**   Am I your conquest, nothing more?
> **John**   Don't force me to be cruel.
> **Julie**   Tell me what I am.
> *Pause.*
> **John**   A fuck. (p. 155)

Writing more than a hundred years after Strindberg, Marber had licence for greater sexual explicitness. Tellingly, in the Strindberg, Kristin deduces that Jean and Julie have had sex but has not actually caught them in the act, whereas Marber has Christine confront John with what she's seen:

> **Christine**   I woke in the night. I opened your door.
> *Pause.*
> You both had your backs to me.
> *Pause.*
> I was wondering if you'd tell me, since we are to be married, for better or worse. (p. 163)

She then asks John 'What was she [Julie] like?'

In just these few lines, her (and Marber's) preoccupation with the physical and qualitative detail of sexual betrayal, and her pre-emptive revelation of her lover's infidelity, link Christine to two moments in *Closer*: Larry's demand in Scene Six for a detailed description from Anna of her sex with Dan, and Dan's interrogation of Alice at the airport hotel, when he has been wondering if Alice would ever tell him about her affair with Larry.

In his Introduction to *Marber Plays: 1*, Richard Eyre
suggests that when Marber wrote his second play,
'Strindberg had leaked into *Closer*'. For Marber himself:
'Doing the Strindberg gave me the territory for a play about
contemporary sexual romantic relationships. Strindberg's
version is more elemental than mine, more about the nature
of man, the nature of woman, which I'm not really
interested in. I'm interested in the specifics of this man, this
woman, this moment.'

Both plays suggest that there is the thinnest of lines
between love and hate. Both expose a vein of cruelty just
beneath the surface of sexual desire: terms of endearment
give way to insults, ice-cold detachment follows the heat of
passion.

'Sexual Perversity in Chicago'
First staged in 1974, David Mamet's *Sexual Perversity in
Chicago* is a short piece made up of more than thirty scenes,
some only a handful of lines long, in which desk-jockeys
Bernard, an obsessively promiscuous misogynist, and
Danny, his younger, less experienced friend, talk incessantly
about tits, blow-jobs and pussy. Danny dates, briefly cohabits with and then separates from commercial artist
Deborah, much to the irritation of her flatmate Joan, a
nursery school teacher, whom Bernard chats up
unsuccessfully in a bar. The language is 'fuck' this and 'cunt'
that, and love is the only four-letter word in short supply.

Marber is a great admirer of Mamet (he has directed *The
Old Neighborhood* and acted in *Speed-the-Plow*; see Chronology),
and acknowledges that *Sexual Perversity* influenced *Closer*'s
four-hander structure and language (the profanity in both
plays is there not for shock value but because this is how
these characters talk about sex). Larry's misogyny does not
run as deep as Bernard's (it's impossible to picture the latter
as a married man, even briefly), but until he settles down
with Anna, he and Bernard both subscribe to the view that
the more women you fuck the better and bigger man you
become. Linguistically, both plays are equally terse, their
dominant rhythm established by characters exchanging

single or half lines; speeches longer than a couple of
sentences are exceptionally rare.

'sex, lies and videotape'
The first film by the American writer and director Steven
Soderbergh, *sex, lies and videotape* (1989) won the Palme d'Or
at the Cannes Film Festival and went on to become one of
the most profitable and influential films in the history of US
independent cinema. Set and shot in Baton Rouge,
Louisiana, it is essentially a four-hander: Anne (Andie
MacDowell) is an insecure, introverted housewife locked in
a stifling marriage to a cocksure lawyer, John (Peter
Gallagher), who is having an affair with Anne's sister, the
sexually assured, extrovert Cynthia (Laura San Giacomo), a
would-be artist who makes ends meet as a barmaid. When
an old college friend of John's, the quietly spoken,
apparently alienated Graham (James Spader), comes to
town and rents a bungalow near John and Anne's house, she
is drawn to his sensitivity, the antithesis of John's alpha-male
strutting. When she finds out that Graham has a collection
of videotaped interviews with women in which they tell him
about their sex lives, she recoils. Cynthia visits Graham and
records a tape of her sexual confessions. After discovering
John and Cynthia's affair, Anne decides to leave him, and
the film ends hopefully, with Anne and Graham in the early
stages of a relationship.

   Apart from a few lines for five minor characters (Anne's
therapist, Graham's landlord, a barfly who lusts after
Cynthia, one of the video interviewees and a work colleague
of John's), the script is, like *Closer*, a four-hander, built
almost entirely from duologues, mostly set in domestic
interiors (John and Anne's home, Cynthia's and Graham's
apartments) – so much so that it's possible to imagine a
successful stage adaptation of the film that would require
minimal alteration to the screenplay.

   Variety magazine reviewed the film as 'a sexy, nuanced,
beautifully controlled examination of how a quartet of people
are defined by their erotic impulses and inhibitions' – a

summary equally applicable to *Closer*. The film made a great impression on Marber: 'I remember seeing it when it came out and just thinking that this was a voice I hadn't heard before. At the time it was about people older than I was. I'd have been in my mid-twenties, but I knew what they were talking about. It was very shocking and very contemporary. Just a film that's always stayed with me. Soderbergh did something there that was very accurate, and haunting, simultaneously realistic and poetic, and I always like that.'

Soderbergh and Marber are both interested in the impact of contemporary technology on sexuality. Through the character of Graham, Soderbergh was tapping into the relatively recent phenomenon of ordinary men and women acquiring affordable and portable video cameras with which they could record and watch their own sex lives (an inevitable consequence of the 1980s explosion in the home video market for professionally made pornographic films shot on the same cameras). The impotent Graham uses his video recordings of women talking about their sexual experiences to achieve orgasm; until he meets Anne, he's been left so damaged by the end of a long-term relationship that he can only find sexual gratification without physical or emotional contact. Almost a decade later, Marber uses the cyberspace encounter between Dan and Larry to show the internet's limitless potential for explicitness without intimacy (watched today, Soderbergh's film only seems dated when Anne worries that Graham might take the videotape of Cynthia masturbating and 'bounce it off some satellite' for the viewing pleasure of strangers; now she'd worry that Graham would upload the footage on to his website).

'When we were rehearsing the film of *Closer* in London, there was a dinner for Soderbergh, who was in town. He and Julia Roberts know each other and I got invited. I was able to say "*Closer* wouldn't have happened without you. Thank you. I was profoundly influenced by your film." Soderbergh then came to see *After Miss Julie* the next night and I was very pleased to give him a copy of the play. *Closer* can be looked at as *Sexual Perversity in Chicago* or *sex, lies and videotape* rewritten. I mean they're all the same play, really.

Each successive generation needs to go: "No, no, this is where love is at the moment." I was lucky that *Closer* sort of did that when I wrote it.'

The extent to which Soderbergh caught the mood of the times was reflected in the way that the film's title entered the vernacular, becoming the basis for countless newspaper and magazine headlines and subheadings in America and Britain that would announce tales of 'sex, lies and politics/sport [insert appropriate noun]'. That resonance chimed directly with *Time Out* magazine's Critics' Choice listings in June 1997, which described *Closer* as follows: 'Sex, lies and the internet explored in Patrick Marber's brilliant new play.'

Fiction or autobiography?
Inevitably, as a thirty-something Londoner writing about the sex lives of thirty-something Londoners, Marber was often asked by journalists if *Closer* was partly or wholly autobiographical. As he told the *Daily Telegraph* theatre critic Charles Spencer in an interview in October 1999: 'The trite answer is that everything is true but none of it happened. It is emotionally true, but the events, the plotting, the narrative, isn't true of my life, though I've experienced most of the emotions experienced by the characters in the play. When you're in your early twenties your love life seems to explode every twenty minutes or so. By the time you've reached your thirties, it is every five or ten years. Jealousy taps you on the shoulder and says "remember me?". Ditto infidelity. To some members of the audience it's a horrible reminder of what they've been through. To others, who are going through this stuff at the same time as they are watching the play, there is a strong element of recognition. I've had letters from people saying, "You've written my life, how did you know?"'

The title
Responding to an audience question at a National Theatre Platform talk on *Closer* in December 1999, Marber admitted:

'The title is stolen. I wish I'd thought of it, but it's the title of Joy Division's second album.' Joy Division were the Manchester band whose most famous song, 'Love Will Tear Us Apart', might have given Marber a subtitle for his play. Their second album was released in 1980, a few months after their lead singer, Ian Curtis, had killed himself, and its songs have been described by the Manchester rock writer Mick Middles as 'the sound of somebody in desperation'. On one track, Curtis sings 'I put my trust in you' in a tone that makes it clear that his loved one has betrayed him.

At the NT Platform, Marber added: 'Joy Division were a band I used to love when I was in my teens. *Closer* was their second album and my second play. I could have called it something like *Love and Other Miseries* but wanted it to resonate outwards. It took me quite a long time to accept it as a title because I wanted to come up with my own, but in the end I couldn't, so stole someone else's.'

It's a perfect title, encompassing the characters' contrasting searches for and reactions to physical and emotional closeness; their doomed attempts at getting closer to another person's heart and soul; and, in a play preoccupied with mortality, the way that every day brings us closer to death. 'The title is absolutely correct in its ambiguity,' Marber says. 'It is the best possible title for the play because the play is always aspiring to get closer to some kind of definitive truth about things but knows it can't.'

At certain moments, one wants to put a question mark after the title. Will Alice let the next man in her life get closer to her real identity than the last? Will a young nurse bring Larry closer than Anna could to the kind of fulfilment he seeks? At other times, you feel the characters would like to make the title an order, for instance, when Anna asks Dan (p. 79), 'When we're making love, why don't you kiss me? Why don't you like it when I say I love you? I'm on your side. *Talk to me.*' She is really saying: 'Closer!'

All those things are going on in the title, agrees Marber, but ultimately the unpredictability of relationships means that: 'If you had to punctuate after it, really it's *Closer . . .*'

Structure and time

Scene	Month/Year	Who's with whom	Who's in the scene
1	Jan., year 0	Dan + Ruth; Alice single; Larry single; Anna separated	Dan, Alice, Larry
2	June, year 1	Dan + Alice; Larry single; Anna separated	Dan, Anna, Alice
3	Jan., year 2	Dan + Alice; Larry single; Anna separated	Dan, Larry
4	Jan., year 2	Dan + Alice; Larry single; Anna separated	Larry, Anna
5	June, year 2	Dan + Alice; Larry + Anna;	Dan, Alice, Larry, Anna
6	June, year 3	Dan + Alice; Larry + Anna; Dan + Anna	Larry, Anna / Dan, Alice
7	Sept., year 3	Dan + Anna; Alice single; Larry single	Larry, Alice
8	Oct., year 3	Dan + Anna; Alice + Larry	Dan, Anna, Larry
9	Nov., year 3	Dan + Anna; Larry + Alice	Alice, Anna, Larry
10	Dec., year 3	Dan single; Alice single; Larry + Anna	Dan, Larry
11	Jan., year 4	Dan + Alice; Larry + Anna	Dan, Alice
12	July, year 4	Larry + Polly; Dan single; Anna single; Alice dead	Anna, Larry, Dan

This chart illustrates the symmetrical, almost musical construction of *Closer*, Marber building the play as a series of linked duets or dances. Indeed, several reviewers of the original production described the play as a quadrille, defined by the dictionaries as a square dance for four couples, containing five sections of figures, each of which is a complete dance in itself. Here, each successive dance helps determine the choreography of the next.

This bruising sequence of human collisions explains why Marber says he chose the Newton's Cradles that Alice gives Dan and Larry as what he calls 'sort of the symbol of the play – albeit an ironic and tacky one'. The four central characters / steel balls knock each other back and forth, with an outsider (Ruth and then Polly) attached in the first and last scenes.

Ultimately, there is so little harmony between the voices and bodies in each song/dance, that *Closer* feels more like a marathon bout of tag-team wrestling. Marber manoeuvres his characters so that even on the six occasions when three or four of them appear in the same scene and location, they are only permitted to share the stage for a few seconds. Dan stays in the ring just long enough after Alice's arrival in Scene Two for her to begin grappling with Anna; in Scene Nine as soon as Alice joins him and Anna in the museum, Larry says 'I think I'll leave you two to it' and exits; and in Scene Twelve, where Larry withdraws from the fray as soon as Dan enters.

This meticulous construction took physical form when Marber was writing: 'I had a pinboard with cards on it and a very big table, and I had different coloured cards and a card for each character and I'd rearrange them on the table and pin them on the board. I had maybe twenty scenes that could have been scenes in the play.

'The thing I knew about *Closer* was that I wanted each scene to have its own depth charge built into it. I tried to construct a play where it didn't really have a beginning, middle and end but each scene did, and, hopefully, it would accumulate.' Each scene has that explosive quality because Marber presents only the sparks that ignite, or reignite, each relationship, and the crises or confrontations that end them, temporarily or for good. The sparks come with Dan and Alice at the hospital; Dan and Anna at her studio and the gallery; Larry and 'Anna' online and Larry and Anna at the Aquarium; Larry and Alice at the lapdance club; Larry telling Dan where to find Alice. The endings come via the revelations of Scenes Six and Eight; Alice reuniting Larry and Anna in Nine; Dan interrogating and hitting

Alice in Eleven; the fatal accident that we learn about in Twelve.

Of the many long time lapses between scenes, Marber says: 'I think that if *Closer* has a problem it's a problem of momentum, that it doesn't necessarily accelerate. In a really good production it does, it seems to drive through to its end, but sometimes I've seen it and it feels like twelve one-scene plays that don't fully add up.'

The contrast between the elegant construction and the rawness of the language and behaviour is one of the keys to *Closer*'s power. As Marber said in his interview with Charles Spencer: 'The idea was always to create something that has a formal beauty into which you could shove all this anger and fury. I hoped the dramatic power of the play would rest on that tension between elegant structure – the underlying plan is that you see the first and last meeting of every couple in the play – and inelegant emotion.'

Countless plays, including Marber's *Dealer's Choice* and *After Miss Julie*, unfold in one location across twenty-four hours or less, observing the classical unities of time and place that, if properly used, give focus and momentum to the action, creating the illusion that everything depicted on stage has happened, in effect, during our evening at the theatre. Other dramatists make vast leaps in time, presenting a crucial action, then pausing to show its long-term consequences, a tactic perhaps most famously deployed by Shakespeare, with the sixteen-year jump between Acts Three and Four in *The Winter's Tale*.

To present a dozen decisive moments in *Closer*'s interlocking relationships, each one marking the start or end of a particular phase, Marber uses an exceptionally flexible timescale, in which the brief gap between one blackout and the lights coming up on the next scene may signal the passage of hours, weeks or months.

Marber has acknowledged the considerable influence of Harold Pinter on his work and in *Closer*'s use of time one can see his clear debt to Pinter's *Betrayal* (1978), which in nine scenes traces the adulterous affair between Jerry, a married literary agent, and Emma, an art gallery owner married to

Jerry's best friend, Robert, a publisher. Pinter's most dazzling stroke was to tell the story largely in reverse order, working backwards from 1977 when Jerry and Emma meet for a drink having not seen each other for a couple of years, to 1968, when, at a party, Jerry first reveals to Emma his passion for her, after which, we deduce, the affair actually began.

Scene One of *Betrayal* takes place in spring 1977 and Two later that season; Three moves to winter 1975, Four to autumn 1974 and Five to the summer of 1973. Scenes Six and Seven follow Five in conventional order, both set progressively later in the summer of 1973. Then we move back to summer 1971 for scene Eight and to the winter of 1968 for Nine. *Closer*'s last scene echoes *Betrayal*'s first (ex-lovers meet to catch up on their now separate lives), and its first echoes Pinter's last (a man and a woman on the brink of an affair).

In both plays, the intervals between scenes are specified in the script, but for the National Theatre premiere of *Closer* the chronology was neither printed in the programme nor flashed up on stage like the captions in a film or television drama, so it was up to the audience to pay close attention to the dialogue to know how long a period had elapsed since the previous scene.

Crucially, because Marber ends most of the scenes with 'cliffhanger' moments, when you first experience *Closer* on stage or film (Mike Nichols eschewed on-screen time captions), its progress is fuelled by engrossing questions, less 'Whodunnit?' than 'Who's-now-with-whom?' Put crudely, it's possible to imagine a 'Tune in next time!' soap opera voiceover asking after Scene Two: 'Will Dan pursue Anna?', or, after Scene Seven: 'Does Alice sleep with Larry?' Our desire to find out what has happened next makes this character-driven play more compelling than many a plot-driven murder-mystery, and time is always an essential element in each new revelation – of an affair begun, interrupted or resumed; we are as keen as the characters to ask 'How long has this been going on?'

In every scene, Marber marks out *Closer*'s calendar and

the peaks and troughs in its relationship chart with great economy, in lines that often serve to pinpoint the timescale for the audience and resolve the 'who's-with-whom?' mystery using the same few words. In the transition from Scene One to Two we move from hearing that Dan always wanted to have written a book to the fact that he's about to have a novel published. Nothing in Scene Three lets us know how much time has passed since Two, or if Dan has seen Anna again, and it's not until Four that we realise how far we have moved on:

> **Anna**   I don't know him [Dan] really, I took his photo for a book he wrote.
> **Larry**   I hope it sank without trace.
> **Anna**   It's on its way. (p. 33)

This should remind us of Dan telling Anna in Scene Two that his novel will be published 'next year', so the exchange confirms that Dan and Anna are not yet lovers and reveals where we are in time. Similarly, the transition to Anna's exhibition in Scene Five should make us think back to her telling Dan in Two that she has an exhibition 'next summer'. That Anna and Larry have become a couple is subtly revealed: 'I'm the Big Fat Liar's boyfriend.' (Larry, p. 38). When Alice tells Larry that they have met before, 'Two and a half years ago' (p. 40), the precise sequence of the first four scenes is all but complete, underlined for the last time by Anna telling Dan, 'I haven't seen you for a <u>year</u>' (p. 43).

The next revelatory 'time-line' comes from Dan in Scene Six: 'I've been with Anna. I'm in love with her. We've been seeing each other for a year' (p. 48), followed, moments later, by belated news that Anna and Larry have married:

> **Larry**   I want to remember this moment for ever: the first time I walked through the door, returning from a business trip, to be greeted by my *wife*. (p. 48)

This is a one-two punch by Marber: we find out that Anna betrayed Larry and only then that they're married.

From Scenes Six to Seven, the gap (extended in

performance by an interval) is measured by Larry's perfectly natural enquiry about Alice's stripping career:

Larry How long you been doing this?
Alice Three months.
Larry Straight after he left you?
Alice No one left me. (p. 63)

To keep track accurately, we need to put this together with the moment in Eight, when Dan asks Anna about her meeting with Larry and is suspicious of her evasive tone because: 'You haven't seen him for four months' (Dan, p. 74). The question of whether Alice and Larry had sex after their meeting in Scene Seven is only answered in Nine, when Anna questions him about the affair:

Anna When did it start?
Larry About a month ago.
Anna <u>Before</u> or <u>after</u> I came to your surgery?
Larry The night before. (p. 85)

As we move towards the end of the play, Marber is less concerned with this pattern of delayed revelation, instead accelerating towards the conclusion with the two most direct scene openings in the play. Scene Ten thus begins with a bald statement of how things have moved on since the museum:

Larry So?
Dan I want Anna *back*. (p. 92)

While in Eleven, no words are needed to let us know that Alice and Dan are back together, simply the stage picture of Dan in bed and then Alice's offstage voice calling from the bathroom. Marber establishes a sense that the play's timespan is drawing to a close, a feeling of events coming full circle, by having the couple relive their first meeting on their fourth anniversary; their talk of sneers and euphemisms is how it began, and how it ends.

Dan hitting Alice puts the full stop to their relationship but at the start of Scene Twelve Marber draws out the last moments of 'Who's with whom?' tension with visual and linguistic echoes of two moments in Larry and Anna's past:

> **Anna**   *Spy.*
> **Larry** *approaches.*
> **Anna**   You've got the coat
> **Larry**   The white coat.

This could be the pair recalling both their first meeting and the moment in Scene Five when he said that he wasn't spying on her but 'Lovingly *observing*' (p. 45). They might still be together – until Anna says: 'How's Polly?' It's an exceptionally powerful effect: in an instant we move from thinking Anna and Larry could still be a couple to hearing of his latest flame. Time has not stood still; they've both moved on yet again.

Finally, the last and most potent revelation:

> **Larry**   How did she die?
> **Anna**   I don't know. When he phoned, he said it happened last night in New York. He's flying out today and he wanted to see us before he left.
> **Larry**   So they weren't together?
> **Anna**   They split up in January.

The bright daylight simulated by the stage lighting and the clothes worn by the actors suggest summer weather (it's warm enough for Larry to be carrying his white coat, not wearing an overcoat), so several months must have gone by since Eleven.

Grouped together like this, Marber's 'time signals' might seem too pointed, but, evenly spaced out in performance, they show a dramatist exploiting theatrical time with great skill. Marber relishes the freedom to make a year pass in a few seconds, just as in Scenes Six and Eight he enjoys making consecutive meetings appear to occur concurrently in the same location (a technique discussed in detail on pp. lxiv–lxv). The four-and-a-half-year span of the play and the uneven intervals between scenes help to demonstrate that Larry's remark to Anna in Scene Six, 'Time: what a tricky little fucker,' alludes to much more than jetlag. Time can play tricks on us, when months and years can go by almost without our realising, and Marber reinforces this feeling by setting three scenes on significant personal milestones (Anna's birthday in Scene Four; Larry's birthday in Nine; Alice and Dan's fourth anniversary in Eleven), reminding us and them of how the years slip through our grasp.

Though the action unfolds chronologically, Marber says that Mike Nichols always viewed the story as retrospective: 'Mike always felt *Closer* was much more about time than anything else. He felt like the whole play exists in memory and what we're watching is everyone remembering Alice. The given of the play for him is that she's dead and Larry, Anna and Dan are eternally stuck in Postman's Park, remembering how they interacted with this girl. I once saw the play in Munich, where the director dropped a gauze for the last scene and they played the whole thing behind it. So you could still see the characters but it was "milky" and it absolutely did that thing with time that Mike was talking about.'

Ultimately, *Closer* dramatises the way in which millions of us recall intimate relationships, not as a day-to-day continuum but as a sequence of moments. 'It's absolutely about that feeling,' says Marber. 'About asking yourself, "How can something that was so real and so potent then, now be just glimpses?" '

It is Alice in Scene Eleven who expresses the most positive attitude to coping with the passage of time and its inevitable final destination:

Dan [. . .] And then you stepped into the road.
It was the moment of my life.
Alice *This* is the moment of your life.

Treat every day, every second as '*the* moment of your life' and you have the best possible chance, if not to defeat time, then to make the most of your allotted span. What irony, therefore, that it is the youngest character and the one whose life is so prematurely cut short who perceives this.

Identity

> Much of the play comes from an anxiety I have about what we
> are. What is a human being? Are we our jobs, our families, our
> blood, our desires? (Patrick Marber)

'Identity is slippery'
Questions of identity are central to *Closer*. Each character's
view of what kind of person they are changes through the
course of the play, confirmed or challenged by the impact
their lovers have on them, and vice versa.

Marber is fascinated by the way that love, passion and the
need for compromise in relationships can demolish men's
and women's apparently secure self-knowledge. Dan, Alice,
Larry and Anna all believe, and at times openly declare,
that they're not the kind of person who would ever take a
particular course of action – steal another man's or woman's
partner, take private patients and live in an elegantly
furnished home, allow a lover to leave them – only to find
themselves doing precisely that. Can we give in to passion,
the play asks, and remain true to who we are, or who we
thought we were?

Marber also suggests that identity may be too complex
and unpredictably protean for us fully to know those
closest to us, especially when a young woman can so
convincingly assume a false identity. 'At the core of the
play there's an idea, very small and unprofound, but
nevertheless an idea, that even with the people that you're
most intimate with, physically and in relationships, can
you ever fully know anyone else? Are we ultimately
condemned to be alone? The line of Dan's, "We live as we
dream, alone", is crucial. Because everyone's identity is
slippery.'

Marber leaves us to provide our own answers to these
questions, because, in his own words, 'I'm not interested in
starting with a single idea and excavating it. I like flicking
out a range of possibilities of meaning and then having
audiences agree or disagree. What I mean is I don't write to

examine a point and have arguments for and against it, the
impulse is much less coherent.'

Dan

Dan undergoes the greatest changes in *Closer*, which is a
principal reason why Marber believes 'it's the most difficult
of the four parts to play'. He starts out as, in Alice's
dismissive phrase, a 'pussy', hamstrung by suburban
convention. 'That's what people do in these situations,' he
tells Alice at the hospital, because he's one of those people.
He defines his private and professional lives by a series of
negatives: he's not the kind of guy who fakes illness to spend
a working day with an attractive stranger, let alone cheat on
his girlfriend with that stranger. He has no talent (p. 9) and
is therefore not going to write novels. His epitaph should be
'reserved' because he withholds more than he gives.

In Scene Two, Marber shows us how Alice has in the
space of eighteen months changed most of Dan's negatives
to positives. He has borrowed and fictionalised her identity
to go from would-be to published novelist, using her wealth
of life experiences to make up for the poverty of his own: the
Woolf devours the waif. To her cost, he has also borrowed
Alice's 'disarming' sexual confidence. The Dan of Scene
One could never have made such a forceful advance on
Anna while he was single, let alone when in a relationship.
In this very economically presented transition, the structure
of *Closer* begins to take shape.

By the gallery scene, Dan is so shocked at what he feels to
be his uncharacteristic behaviour that he no longer
recognises himself, telling Anna: 'This is not me, I don't do
this' (p. 44), and as he leaves Alice in Scene Six, he
acknowledges that she has changed his life (p. 54).

Marber says: 'Alice brings Dan back to life. Because he's
back to life he writes a book and because he writes a book
he gets to meet Anna and because he's been loved by Alice
he has the confidence to seduce Anna. The irony for Alice,
of course, is that she gives him the strength to leave her. But
this happens all the time: "When I met you, you were

nothing." "I know, but because of you I'm strong enough to do without you and choose someone better." I suspect this has been going on since people lived in caves.'

Dan's passion for both women, the confidence it gives him and the pain that the loss of Anna causes him all combine to distort his emotional logic to the point where it costs him his second chance with Alice. When at the hotel she asks why he is testing her and he replies, 'Because I'm an idiot' (p. 107), he knows that he has no right to resent Alice's relationship with Larry; there was no betrayal to match his during the affair with Anna, and yet he can't help himself.

The concluding irony for Dan is that no matter how different a person he has become, in Scene Twelve he is back to square one. Notes Marber: 'His life changes a huge amount, from being Mr Obituary Hack to potentially happening novelist, to failure, to back to being on obits and being the editor, condemned to that thing he wanted to escape.'

Alice
Alice's pin-sharp vision of her self is one of the things that disarms Dan in Scene One. She's so different from him, so certain. Unlike Dan, she does not need rules (lighting up in the hospital) or possessions (everything she needs is in a rucksack); this is a classic example of opposites attracting.

The brief exchange about her ex-boyfriend is important not just because it gives Dan encouraging evidence that she's single, but because it informs us that she defines herself by an ethical code that will prove as durable as Dan's, Larry's and Anna's prove fragile. Dan asks how she can have run away from her companion so abruptly:

> **Dan**   Just like that?
> **Alice**   It's the only way to leave; 'I don't love you any more, goodbye.'
> **Dan**   Supposing you do still love them?
> **Alice**   You don't leave. (p. 13)

Marber is already preparing us for Scene Six, when the

foundations of Alice's romantic life are destroyed by Dan's infidelity. She starts to leave him, but can't because she still loves him, and is left floundering:

> **Alice** Why isn't love enough?
> I'm the one who leaves.
> I'm supposed to leave *you*.
> *I'm* the one who leaves. (pp. 54–5)

This baffled repetition shows how Dan has shattered her sense of self, forcing her into a role she never envisaged playing.

Yet she will, ultimately, be the one who leaves for good, doing to Dan what she did to the boyfriend in America:

> **Alice** I've left . . . I've *gone*.
> 'I don't love you any more. Goodbye.' (p. 106)

And she leaves.

Marber: 'That relates to Dan having asked her in Scene One: "You've never left someone you still love?" She says no, but I think her journey in the play is that sometimes you have to. In *Dealer's Choice*, the poker player, Ash, says to the father, Stephen: "Bit like aces, kids, I suppose. You fall in love with them, you can't pass . . ." and Stephen replies: "Yuh . . . sometimes you have to" [Marber, *Plays: 1*, p. 118]. Stephen knows that in the next scene he is going to sort of forsake his son. Somewhere in both plays I'm exploring a theme: that the terrible thing you have to recognise is that even though you love someone you have to abandon them.'

The sense that what Dan hears from Alice is an absolute and enduring truth about how she lives her life is most strongly affirmed when we hear that she's been knocked down and killed in New York, and recall her saying 'I never look where I'm going' (p. 7). She dies as she lived.

The irony underpinning Alice's truthfulness and rigid moral code is that the superficial definition of her identity – her name – is an invention: Alice Ayres was really plain Jane Jones after all. This final revelaton of Alice's 'identity fraud' presents the play's most negative response to Marber's question: 'Can you ever fully know someone else?' If you

can share your life with a woman for years and not even
know her real name, then the answer must be 'no'.

The final scene also makes it clear, in retrospect, that
Larry had already seen through her disguise on his birthday
visit to Postman's Park in Scene Nine:

> **Larry**   . . . I walked through Postman's Park to get here . . .
> and I had a little look . . . at the memorial.
> **Alice**   Oh.
> **Larry**   Yeah . . . *oh*. (p. 82)

This 'clinical observer of the human carnival' has accepted
this merely as one more among many deceptions, and
carried on with the relationship. That he does not tell Anna
or Dan about Alice/Jane is understandable on grounds both
of character (how delightful for Larry to crush Dan in Scene
Ten by telling him that he is fucking Alice and still have in
reserve the secret pleasure of knowing more about her than
the younger man or his wife) and, more importantly,
dramatic expediency (Marber would not want to ruin the
impact of his last-scene revelation).

Thanks to Dan's novel, there is a third version of
Alice/Jane to contend with: the one Dan has fictionalised
from Alice's accounts of her life:

> **Larry**   It's about *you*, isn't it?
> **Alice**   Some of me.
> **Larry**   Oh? What did he leave out?
> *Beat.*
> **Alice**   The truth. (pp. 39–40)

'This third Alice is entirely bogus,' says Marber, 'a notional
identity who Jane has invented and who's much racier than
Jane and much racier than Alice in a way.' Trying to define
a loved one's identity in print, therefore, is no more likely to
yield the whole truth than sexual or conversational
intimacy.

Larry

Larry's self-knowledge seems rock-solid at the start of the

play. 'He seems to be the most centred of the characters,' says Marber, 'but changes as he deals with all kinds of class, money and status anxieties.' In his sex life (also discussed on pp. xliv–xlvi), he adheres to his promiscuous instincts by pursuing as many women as he can. Indeed, on the evidence Marber provides, Larry's sexual impulses appear to outweigh all else, right from his brief appearance in Scene One and a stage direction that gives the actor a strong introductory moment: '*He is about to walk away. He glances briefly at Alice "Pretty girl". He stops*' (p. 11). That we are watching a doctor who'll never let medical obligation take precedence over an opportunity to chat to an attractive woman (real or virtual) will be confirmed in Scene Three when: '*Larry's phone rings. He picks up the receiver and replaces it without answering. Then he takes it off the hook*' (p. 28); and in the Aquarium, the urge to pursue a new, unexpected sexual opportunity immediately vanquishes the shame and embarrassment that would have sent many other men retreating sheepishly as soon as they realised that Anna was not 'Anna'. He exits, but swiftly returns, insisting, 'NO. We spoke on the Net but now you've *seen* me you don't [want to have sex with me] . . . it's *fine*, I'm not going to get upset about it' (p. 32). It's his vanity that's been wounded, not any sense of propriety; we know that he's a caveman long before he describes himself as one, but he knows it too.

This trait is underlined for the last time in Scene Twelve, the third time that we meet him on NHS, rather than private duty, when he exits as soon as Dan enters. On this occasion, having patients to see gives him an excuse not to confront any grief he might feel over Alice's death and the messy aftermath of his contact with Anna and Dan. Unlike in Scenes One and Three, there's no sexual advantage to be gained by keeping patients or colleagues waiting, so he doesn't.

The other dominant factor in his identity is class: he's in a middle-class profession but, initially, has affirmed his roots by not accepting middle-class private patients. In the NT Studio draft, Marber originally emphasised this characteristic at the Aquarium, with Larry telling Anna how as a medical student: 'I was a pugnacious, chippy little fucker and I wanted to beat the honking Sloanes at their own game.'

Just as Alice changes Dan, so Anna takes Larry up the social scale in how he dresses and where he lives. If he's sleeping with an acclaimed photographer, it's more natural to trade up to private practice, to become 'a sell-out' (p. 41). The son of a cab driver wears cashmere for the first time and feels like 'Cinderella at the ball', and the class dynamic is encapsulated in just two lines:

> **Anna** (*charmed*)   You're such a peasant!
> **Larry**   You love it. (p. 46)

The sense that it's a good thing for her to be slumming it and him to be sleeping above his station is then devastatingly undermined:

> **Anna**   You seem more like 'the cat who got the cream'. You can stop licking yourself, you know.
> *Pause.* **Anna** *turns to* **Larry**, *slowly.*
> **Larry** (*coolly*)   That's the nastiest thing you've ever said to me. (p. 47)

The tension between their backgrounds peaks in Scene Six, when Larry speaks of the *Elle Decoration* bathroom being cleaner than he is:

> **Anna**   You chose it.
> **Larry**   Doesn't mean I like it. We shouldn't have . . . *this.*
> **Larry** *gestures vaguely about the room.*
> **Anna**   Are you experiencing bourgeois guilt?
> *Beat.*
> **Larry** (*sharp*)   Working-class guilt. (pp. 50–1)

Was he trying to assuage this guilt and sabotage his 'undeserved' marriage by having sex with the hooker in New York, or following his caveman instincts, or both?

Ultimately, his response to his new girlfriend Polly's jokey ultimatum – 'She said she wouldn't have sex with me until I gave up private medicine. What's a man to do?' (p. 111) – proves that in his internal battle the caveman will always

defeat the assumed persona of upwardly mobile 'sell-out'.
He knows this, and has ruefully succumbed to self-
knowledge; Anna knows it, too:

Larry   Everyone learns, nobody changes.
Anna   *You* don't change. (p. 110)

Marber says there are elements here of the John/Julie
relationship in *After Miss Julie* (discussed in more detail on
pp. xvi–xix). 'Anna is a cut above those Larry has had
before and he's slightly intimidated by who she is and where
she comes from and enjoys that intimidation. I've always
thought of Larry that he goes on this little trip and he
plunges into the bourgeois world and the world of marriage
and commitment and gets badly burnt and retreats back to
being the fucking bachelor. What he discovers is that
actually "I think I like being a doctor in the NHS and
fucking as many people as I possibly can. And that's who I
am." At the end it's a kind of defeat and retreat and a kind
of rueful acknowledgement of his true self.'

Anna
Until she finally begins the affair with Dan, Anna seems
confident about her professional and social status, and yet
her apparently secure sense of self is defined by a series of
negatives. She is not beautiful (p. 18), does not 'kiss strange
men' or want trouble with Alice and is incapable of stealing
Dan (pp. 20, 22, 25). When she weeps at the Aquarium she
tells Larry she is not permitted to cry. When transformed by
passion into the kind of woman who does lie to her husband
and steal another woman's partner, she finds herself
'disgusting' (p. 56). What never changes is her deep-rooted
fear of conflict and yearning for gentleness, in and out of
bed. Larry and Dan view the former quality as cowardice:
Larry calls her a coward for not telling him about Dan the
moment he arrives home from the airport (p. 57), and Dan
says that she's a coward for not having the guts to let Larry
hate her (p. 78).
     Marber: 'In rehearsals and in talking to directors of

foreign productions I would say that Anna is the heart of the play, Alice is the soul, Dan's the brains and Larry's the balls. We also used to talk in archetypes: Anna is the queen, Dan is the prince, Alice is a princess and Larry is a knight.'

Through the course of the play, she attempts to take control of a life that has hitherto cast her in the role of victim: her first husband left her for someone younger and, in Scene Five, she reveals that she has 'been hit before', whether by her ex or another man. Falling for Dan enables her to take a more active, aggressive role: first by leaving Larry for the younger Dan (reversing what happened in her first marriage), then by returning to Larry. But Marber makes her come full circle: abandoned by Larry for 'someone younger', this time Polly, the nurse. All her lovers conform to her belief that 'men are crap' and beneath her defiance in Scene Twelve:

> **Larry** Don't become . . . a sad person.
> **Anna** I won't. I'm *not*. <u>Fuck off</u>. (p. 111)

must lie the fear that her losing streak will never end. She has come full circle, once again abandoned by a husband, and so have the others: Dan is back at the obituaries desk, weighed down by unfulfilled ambition; Larry is back in the NHS, a happy bachelor sharing his bed with a nurse; Alice has again been involved in a road accident, this time fatally.

Marber: 'The play is often perceived as pessimistic, though my argument is that all three of them come through the fire and might do things better next time. And I really like what the plaque says, and how it is also true of Jane Jones: "saved three children from a burning house in Union Street, Borough, at the cost of her own young life".'

Professional identities

All four characters work in fields where the contact they have with their subjects, patients or customers is superficial and often fleeting, requiring them – at first glance – to give nothing of their true selves.

Dan toils in the remotest, loneliest and least intimate

branch of journalism, the only one that does not require you to meet people, and in which you can only ever write about someone once. Had Marber made Dan not an obituarist but, for instance, a political correspondent whose work depended on developing long-term relationships with MPs, spin doctors and civil servants, his profession would send out very different signals about his character. And yet he does form a strong bond with his boss, Harry Masters (see p. lix), who he hasn't noticed is in love with him, so there *is* intimacy around the obits desk.

As a photographer, Anna is preoccupied with surfaces and the superficial expression of emotion. She takes pictures of strangers whom she need never meet again – the photographic equivalent of one-night stands. Even though she knows Alice's name and has spent time with her, her portrait is anonymously labelled 'Young woman, London'. Alice jokingly asks if Anna has stolen Dan's soul by photographing him (p. 22), but the identity of Anna's subjects seems remote and unknowable, and she need not reveal anything of herself in her work. Marber: 'It's true that Anna has issues with intimacy and explores them in her work. In photographing strangers and then derelict buildings, she's exploring an emptiness in herself through her work, and she knows it.'

As a dermatologist, Larry is called in only when the human surface, the skin, becomes damaged or diseased. He is as preoccupied with our 'ferocious' flesh (p. 97) in his working day as in his sex life. And yet Marber makes clear, through his key speech to Dan about *dermatitis artefacta* in Scene Ten, that Larry is also concerned with the innermost workings of the human heart and mind; the source of skin diseases may be hidden far beneath the surface, and to understand and treat the symptoms, he might sometimes have to probe as deeply as a psychiatrist.

Alice is a stripper whose clients are by definition interested only in her flesh; they want to know her body, not her personality. She can earn good money by showing them every inch without having to have sex with them or reveal anything of her self. The wig adds another layer of protective disguise, but Larry thinks that he sees through her and her colleagues: 'You're all protecting your identities'; and shortly afterwards: '. . . you all use "stage names" to con yourselves you're someone else so you don't feel *ashamed* when you show your <u>cunts</u> and <u>arseholes</u> to Complete Fucking Strangers' (p. 69).

Can stripping really be, as she suggests, an enjoyably empowering means to an end for Alice (it pays for her and Dan's anniversary holiday and gives her a thoroughgoing knowledge of what men want), with no negative side effects on plain Jane Jones's more vulnerable personality? Or perhaps we should conclude that the longer she goes on stripping, the more she needs Dan (or another man) to give her the fidelity, physical and emotional intimacy that is both forbidden and impossible with all the men who come to the club? Marber, of course, provides no simple answers to either question.

When *Closer* opened, a number of critics felt that Marber's choice of professions for his characters was overly schematic, too closely related to the themes of the play and therefore unrealistically contrived. 'It does look schematic,' he says, 'but I'd never thought about it in that way. The professions came from the opening premise, and were defined by the accident at the beginning. There is an accident; he takes her to a hospital, where they meet a doctor and then he gets successful as a novelist. Anna could have been a publisher or editor but for their meeting I wanted a scene that had a bit more activity in it, so I made her a photographer, it wasn't really any deeper than that.'

Sex and love

> Some critics put forward a version of the play in which the men seem to know all about sex and the women are innocent. But it's much more complicated than that. (Patrick Marber)

Though the four sexual relationships dramatised in *Closer* all fail, each couple has enjoyed what Larry in Scene Five calls '<u>Paradise</u>' – the 'first flush' in which, as Marber puts it, 'the

couples have fun and a lot of very pleasurable sex'. Yet
because these honeymoon periods have run their course
largely beyond our gaze, in the intervals between scenes
dominated by confrontations between lovers or sexual rivals,
what emerges more strongly from the play is the impression
of an apparently unbridgeable gulf between male and
female attitudes to love and sex.

Dan and Larry do not begin the play solely fixated on
sexual possession and quantifiable performance. But the
failure of their romantic relationships and, in particular,
their disabling grief and anger at losing Anna as a loving
and beloved partner, leads them to behave more and more
like 'cavemen'. Sex is eventually reduced to a fiercely
competitive, winner-takes-all business, which seems only
loosely connected to emotional intimacy, and the two men
seem incapable of accommodating the more complex needs
of Alice and Anna, who want sex and love to be linked as
closely as possible, but can separate them at will. This most
divisive element in the play is best defined by Anna to Alice
in Scene Nine: 'They spend a lifetime fucking and never
know how to make love' (Anna, p. 90).

Though Dan, even at his most confident, is less of a
'CAVEMAN' than Larry, Marber makes it clear that both
men's take on sex hinges on whether the woman reaches
orgasm, and both believe their prowess is solely responsible
for her climax; if she doesn't come he fails. Marber weaves
this thread throughout the script, beginning with Alice in
Scene One:

> **Alice**   Men want a girl who looks like a boy.
> They want to protect her but she must be a survivor.
> And she must <u>come</u> . . . like a *train* . . . but with . . .
> <u>elegance</u>. [. . .]
> **Dan**   What do *you* want?
> **Alice**   To be loved.
> **Dan**   That simple?
> **Alice**   It's a big want. (p. 14)

Conflicting male/female priorities are immediately
established, and when we move into the simulated online

encounter, Dan, who has learned from Alice, knows that Larry will be disappointed unless he makes 'Anna' masturbate herself to an orgasm indicated (hilariously so, in performance) by 'I'm cumming right now . . .' and the long stream of 'ohohoh . . .' (p. 28).

Stealing two of Alice's phrases from Scene One ('don't be a pussy' and 'cum like a train'), Dan, suggests Marber, 'is getting off on pretending to be "porno Anna", which, clearly, from her behaviour, she is not. Larry knows that there isn't literally a woman having an orgasm at the other end of this virtual conversation. What he's enjoying is the fact that there appears to be a woman out there who's dirty enough to say that she *is* coming. He knows that they're playing a game, and "she" knows they're playing a game, and he hopes that if she's prepared to be dirty online then she'll be dirty in life.'

Their exchange contains another very telling moment: when Larry reveals that he masturbates about ex-girlfriends, never his current partner (p. 28), it hints at a sexual personality allergic to long-term monogamy and primed for infidelity and a string of relationships, because there's always 'better' sex out there than what you're getting now. His behaviour in the rest of the play bears this out.

Beneath the wild comedy of the cybersex exchange (discussed in detail on pp. lxii–lxiv) are the unsettling truths it reveals about the two men's attitudes to women. To amuse himself, Dan adopts the language of heterosexual film pornography, whose 'heroines' crave nothing more than group sex with strangers, including simultaneous vaginal and anal penetration:

> **Dan** They form a Q and I attend to them like a cum hungry bitch, 1 in each hole and both hands.
> **Larry** Then?
> **Dan** They cum in my mouth arse tits cunt hair.

'Cum hungry bitches' could be the title of a porn film or website, as Marber notes: 'Dan, fixated on Anna as he is, is imagining a porno version of Anna who puts herself out on the net. He's thinking himself into her skin, were she as

sexually voracious as he knows she's *not*. He's half abusing
some idiot who he's online with and half getting turned on
by it, and on a good night in the theatre at a certain point
for Dan the joke isn't funny any more because he's sitting
there with a hard-on; the joke's on him to a certain extent. I
conceived that scene to be a rather disturbing erotic
encounter but the way it played was comedic.'

The influence of pornography continues into Scene Four.
When Larry greets Anna in the Aquarium and thinks that
the previous evening's promise of instant sex with an
alluring stranger is to be fulfilled, his excited response, 'I
can't believe these things actually *happen*', is couched in the
language of the letters (supposedly) sent in by readers of
men's magazines such as *Forum*, whose accounts of sex
between strangers have often begun: 'I never thought
something like this would happen to me.'

The obsession with orgasm and sexual visualisation are
particularly shocking in Scene Six (from Larry: 'Did you
come?' to Anna: 'We do everything that people who have
sex do.'), when establishing the fact of Anna's infidelity is
not enough for Larry; he must know every detail. As he
demands to know locations and positions, a film of Anna
and Dan's sex begins to take shape; Anna equips him with
the shooting script that will enable him to edit the footage
together in his mind's eye.

In the next scene Marber returns to this theme – of how
women feed male sexual imagery and how that imagery
influences their behaviour in bed – by making Larry
generalise:

> **Larry**   But you <u>do</u> give us something of yourselves: you give
> us . . . *imagery* . . . and we do with it what we will.
> If you women could see one minute of our Home Movies – the
> shit that slops through our minds every day – you'd string us
> up by our balls, you really would. (p. 72)

In pornography and in lapdancing clubs women are
objectified, denied any real existence other than as bodies
for male sexual gratification, and this motif resurfaces in
Marber's references to prostitution. Beyond the confines of

Closer, women pay gigolos and use pornography; within the world of the play these are transactions with an exclusively male clientele.

Larry pays to see Alice strip and has paid for sex in New York (p. 55). Gradually, we sense that he views all sex on the same terms: the anonymous internet hook-up, the New York whore, or even his wife.

> **Larry**   I treat you like a whore?
> **Anna**   Sometimes. (p. 58)

And when he invites Anna to his surgery in Scene Eight he says, 'Be my whore and in return I will pay you with your liberty' (p. 76). To broken-hearted Larry the female body comes to exist as a chattel to be bought and sold, whereas Marber shows women viewing sex and sexual gratification very differently, as something in their gift, in the process firing some barbed volleys against male vanity.

In Scene Eight, after Anna has admitted screwing Larry at his surgery, Marber has her deliver the *coup de grâce*:

> **Dan**   Did you come?
> **Anna**   No.
> **Dan**   Did you fake it?
> **Anna**   Yes.
> **Dan**   Why?
> **Anna**   To make him *think* I enjoyed it, why do you think?
> **Dan**   If you were just his _slag_ why did you give him the pleasure of thinking you'd enjoyed it?
> **Anna**   Because that's what slags *do*.
> **Dan**   You fake it with me?
> **Anna**   Yes, yes I do. I fake one in three, all right?
> **Dan**   Tell me the truth.
> *Pause.*
> **Anna**   *Occasionally* . . . I have faked it.
> It's not important, you don't *make* me come. I come . . .
> You're . . . 'in the area' . . . providing valiant assistance.
> **Dan**   You make *me* come.
> **Anna**   You're a man, you'd come if the tooth fairy winked at you.

This is a wonderfully rich exchange, as serious as it is comic (in performance, Anna's 'valiant assistance' and 'tooth fairy' lines consistently drew some of the play's loudest laughs). Dan's enquiry echoes Larry's in Scene Six, confirming their shared obsession with the female orgasm. If Anna had *really* reached orgasm at the surgery, Larry's victory would have been complete; according to Dan's warped logic, because she faked it he may have lost a battle but can still win the war.

Anna's sarcastic suggestion that she fakes every third orgasm mocks the male view of sex as a contact sport in which performance is measurable by statistics (in such terms Dan is like a rugby player who only converts every third penalty kick). To Dan and Larry, the female orgasm is something to be won; for Alice and Anna it's entirely in their gift.

At the restaurant, Dan's questioning of Anna echoes Larry's interrogation of Anna in Scene Six:

> **Dan** I love you and I don't like other men <u>fucking</u> you, is that so weird?
> **Anna** No. YES. It was only <u>sex</u>.
> **Dan** (*hard*) If you can still fuck him you haven't left him. (*Softly.*) It's gone . . . we're not innocent any more.
> **Anna** Don't stop loving me ... I can see it draining out of you. (pp. 79–80)

Marber repeats the effect again in Scene Eleven when Dan forces from Alice her redundant confession that she has slept with Larry, 'I fucked Larry. Many times. I enjoyed it. I came. I prefer *you*. Now go' (p. 106).

The women can treat sex according to shifting context, at times in isolation from love, at others as an integral part of a loving relationship. Anna insists, 'I love *you*, I didn't give *him* anything', and calls what happened with Larry 'a mercy fuck' or a '*sympathy* fuck', a form of '*kindness*', not betrayal. Dan disagrees violently. The sex at Larry's surgery and Alice's orgasms with Larry during their affair mean far more to Dan than to either woman, because they love him, not Larry.

His reactions call to mind Dan and Anna's conversation

in Scene Two, when his and Alice's sex with other partners was still hypothetical and he believed Alice was 'completely unleavable':

> **Anna**   And you don't want someone else to get their dirty hands on her?
> *Beat.*
> **Dan**   Maybe.
> **Anna**   Men are crap.
> **Dan**   But all the same . . .
> **Anna**   They're still crap. (p. 21)

This may not be the most poetic or profound analysis of male sexual jealousy, but Anna ultimately concludes that Dan has lived down to her low expectations of all men. In Scene Eight, ignoring Dan's vigorous denials, she persuades herself that his love for her meant nothing more than exclusive sexual possession, and being the only lover to make her come, and thus concludes that, if their relationship is built on such shallow foundations, Larry might offer her a more solid future after all:

> **Anna**   (*tough*)   Why did you swear eternal love when all you wanted was a fuck?
> **Dan**   I didn't just want a fuck, I wanted you.
> **Anna**   You wanted excitement, love bores you.
> **Dan**   No . . . it disappoints me. (p. 80)

Soon afterwards, Marber uses Anna and Alice's confrontation in Scene Nine to demonstrate that, although they may not be as preoccupied by the quantity and quality of orgasms as the men eventually become, the women of *Closer* are just as competitive in their pursuit of sex and love:

> **Alice**   She even looks beautiful when she's angry. The Perfect Woman.
> **Anna**   JUST FUCKING STOP IT.
> **Alice**   Now we're talking. (p. 88)

'Scene Nine is key to the meaning of the play,' Marber says. 'The women are every bit as jealous – and flawed – as the men.'

Anna   Why *now*, why come for me *now*?
Alice   Because I felt strong enough, it's taken me five months
to convince myself you're not better than me.
Anna   It's not a competition.
Alice   <u>Yes it is.</u> (p. 88)

They leave Dan not because the sexual thrill has died, or
because they will find more passion with someone else, but
because of love:

Anna   If you love me enough you'll forgive me. (p. 80)

Alice   *Show me.* Where is this 'love'?
I can't see it, I can't *touch* it, I can't *feel* it. (p. 107)

Death

For a play in which no one is murdered, *Closer* has an
alarmingly high body count.

Death is never far from consideration in the script: as a
visual symbol, Postman's Park was constantly in view in
Vicki Mortimer's design for the National Theatre
production, her upstage facsimile of the commemorative
tablets creating a *memento mori* backdrop to every scene; no
matter what the characters were doing, death, literally and
metaphorically, was hanging over them.

As to the significance that Marber might want us to
attach to the deaths commemorated in the park, it is
ambiguous at best. Elizabeth Boxall (p. 109), the real Alice
Ayres (p. 112) and the rest sacrificed themselves so that
others might live, one death defying Death. Their selfless
acts contrast with the selfishness of all the characters. Yet
their own existences were abruptly, violently cut short, so
are their actions a source of consolation or regret?

The morbid preoccupation begins with Alice's enquiries
on learning where Dan works (p. 6):

Alice   Do you like it … in the *dying* business?
Dan   It's a living.
Alice   Did you grow up in a graveyard?
Dan   Yeah. Suburbia.

continues with her throwaway yet resonant remark a minute or two later:

Alice   How old [are you]?
Dan   Thirty-five.
Alice   Half-time?
Dan   Thank you very much. (p. 8)

and will end with news of her death reaching us in the final scene.

'One of the things that's happening in the play is the characters' increasing consciousness of their own mortality,' says Marber. His creations, especially Larry and Dan, crave the vital sensations of sex as the antithesis – though sadly not the antidote – to death. In pleading for Anna to come away with him at the gallery, Dan even argues that death entitles us to be selfish, that inconsiderate acts may be better for your health: 'Don't give me "kind". "Kind" is *dull*, "kind" will kill you,' and then, at his most desperate: 'I can't think, I can't work, I can't *breathe*. We are going to *die*.' (p. 44).

'When he says "We're going to die" it's a key line for the play,' notes Marber. 'He's inviting her to go to his dad's funeral as a romantic tryst. Gothic writers might have liked that moment. Noël Coward's *Private Lives*, which has two men, two women and the swapping of partners, was a key influence on the shape of *Closer*. In that play there's a very striking remark of Elyot's when he says to his ex-wife, Amanda: "Let's savour the delight of the moment. Come and kiss me darling, before your body rots, and worms pop in and out of your eye sockets" [Coward, *Collected Plays: Two*, Methuen, 1979, p. 57]. One of the cores of the play is "We're going to die, so let's be selfish and get whatever we can while we're here." A lot of the sex in the play is charged with fear of death: "Let's fuck and we might feel a bit more alive as we do so." ' Marber's characters are people who would appreciate the French euphemism for orgasm as *le petit mort*, the little death.

Dan's preoccupation with death is as much professional as personal. His office is a journalistic mortuary in which his colleague Graham asks each morning 'Who's on the slab?'

(p. 10). Yet the subjects of the obituaries are remote figures within the world of the play, background accompaniment to the major theme, in which the deaths of those closest to the characters are never 'good' ones, the deceased slipping peacefully away at a ripe old age, surrounded by loving relations.

When Dan mentions his mother, the implication of: 'She died *here*, actually. <u>She</u> was a smoker' (p. 9) is that she succumbed painfully in hospital to a smoking-related illness, lung cancer, perhaps, or emphysema. Marber, a smoker himself, sees smoking as 'a tiny metaphor running through the play'. Dan has stopped smoking but starts again under Alice's influence; Larry watches Alice smoke at the exhibition opening and tries to deter her, having given up himself, observing: 'Pleasure and self-destruction, the perfect poison' (p. 39). Marber had touched on the same theme in Act Three, Scene Three of *Dealer's Choice*, when the restaurant owner, Stephen, tells one of the poker players that he's only allowed to smoke outside, and adds, 'I've always thought it's a rather interesting tell . . . smoking. Who wants to live, who wants to die?' (Marber, *Plays: 1*, p. 90). 'It's an interesting thing if you're a smoker, it will kill you,' Marber told the National Theatre Platform on *Closer* in 1999. 'It's a pleasing metaphor: that we all do things that are self-destructive, whether we're smokers or not.'

In the same scene, we learn that Dan's father, who has been 'clinging on' to life in a nursing home, has died unmourned by a son who, if not quite hating him, does not care.

Anna   Your father died?
Dan   It's fine, I hated him – no, I didn't – I don't <u>care</u>, I *care* about <u>THIS</u>. (pp. 43–4)

And moments earlier we have learned that Alice's parents died violently:

Alice   When I was eight . . . some metal went into my leg when my parents' car crashed . . . when they *died*. (p. 41)

In the NT Studio draft, Marber took this defining moment
in Alice's past much further (assuming that it actually
happened, despite the New York police in Scene Twelve
having 'no record of her parents' death'). She tells Larry
that one day as they were driving home:

> **Alice**   My parents were having an argument and I was
> screaming 'shut up shut up shut up', and my mother turned
> round and she went 'Alice, shut up' and I said 'Fuck off', and
> there was this terrible silence and my father turned round, he
> was quite scary, he was an electrician, he said 'Where did you
> learn a word like that?', he was really furious. And I said, 'I
> didn't know it was a bad word.'
> *Beat.*
> Then we crashed.

Had Marber retained this speech, it would have given
audiences a comfortable handle on Alice, the chance to
weigh her down with guilt over her parents' demise and
conclude that: 'Of course she behaves like this because she's
traumatised by causing her parents' deaths.' Denied this
easy option, Alice remains inscrutable to us and to Larry,
Dan and Alice, while her parents' deaths join all the others
in defiance of rational explanation. And Marber stresses that
Larry is 'completely wrong' in Scene Ten, when he
confidently tells Dan that Alice's scar was the result of self-
harm after being orphaned, something that is 'fairly
common in children who lose their parents young'. 'Alice
tells Dan the truth,' says Marber. 'She got the scar when she
fell off her bike, refusing to use stabilisers.'

Harry Masters is another to suffer, and his demise gives
us one of the blackest jokes in the play, as we learn that Dan
has earned a 'dead man's shoes' promotion:

> **Larry**   Busy?
> **Dan** (*nods*)   I was made editor.
> **Larry**   Yeah? How come?
> **Dan**   The previous editor died.
> *They smile.*
> Alcohol poisoning. I sat with him for a week, in the hospital.
> (p. 98)

Finally there is Alice herself, knocked down and killed in her prime. Again, Marber does not give his characters or audiences someone to blame; there is no opportunity to distract from grief or loss by channelling it into anger at a perpetrator. A less forceful dramatist might have softened the ending by letting Dan rage against, say, a drunk-driver for killing Alice. Instead, death in *Closer* is just *there*, random, inevitable. Death's only consolation, if that is the right word, is that the emotional pain the characters cause each other, and the physical or emotional agonies that may lie in store for the surviving trio after the end of the play, is finite:

Larry Thank God life *ends* – We'd never survive it. (p. 97)

Chance

As *Closer* ends, audiences are left with an overwhelming sense that whom we fall in love with is as much a matter of chance as conscious choice or compatibility. The story begins and ends with actual accidents, the clash of metal on flesh and bone; in between, the collisions involving the four principals seem no less haphazard. We may control our lives through choosing to stay with or abandon a lover, but the paths we find ourselves on are laid down by chance.

It is pure chance that Dan happens to be passing as Alice is knocked down. Dan's publishers might have commissioned a male photographer, instead of Anna, just as Ruth's husband's publishers might have sent his poems to a male translator; neither couple would ever have met. When Anna asks Larry how his affair with Alice began, he replies vaguely: 'I went to a club, she happened to be there' (p. 85).

The least plausible, and funniest, coincidence sees Anna's visit to the Aquarium overlap with Larry's, and perhaps the most banal comes in the play's final moments:

Dan She told me that she fell in love with me because . . . I cut off my crusts . . . but it was just… it was only that day . . . because the bread . . . broke in my hands. (p. 114)

The pair just happen to meet on the day when the bread

happens to break and Dan's crustless sandwiches are the quirk that, in Marber's words, 'gave Alice her "in" for a relationship. The sandwiches were not as casual as Dan thinks. Because he cut off his crusts she fell in love with the idea of falling in love with him.'

Marber concedes that the Aquarium scene depends on a 'lethal' degree of contrivance: 'It is a magnificent coincidence – though less so on stage than in the film of *Closer*. On screen it seems ludicrously coincidental. In a theatre the coincidence is somehow allowable because there are only four people and London is laid out before them and anything can happen – it's my version of the Forest of Arden in *As You Like It*, a magical place. Whereas in the film London is actually there in front of your eyes.' The London of *Closer* on stage is, inevitably, indistinct and allusive, in the film it is a literal, real place (see pp. lviii; lxxv–lxxviii).

Yet he suggests that he dramatises nothing more or less plausible than real life: 'When I directed the play and started talking to the actors and asked them to tell me some coincidences that have happened in their lives, it poured out of them. So, yes, the Aquarium is very dodgy and yet not dodgy at all, because it happens all the time. Anna's got a very good reason for being in the Aquarium at that time, it's her birthday, she's taking photos, which we know she's done before. There are struts supporting the coincidence. I'm not ashamed of ludicrous coincidence. Because somewhere the play is arguing that who we love is random, chancy, not star-crossed destiny. But I don't think that's an anti-romantic position to adopt. It just strikes me as true.'

Like any dramatist, Marber has to bring his characters together somehow; just as Shakespeare must make Romeo go to the Capulet ball in *Romeo and Juliet*, because if the hero stays at home sulking we do not have a play. Marber chooses to manoeuvre his protagonists along paths filled with coincidence, but he would argue, rightly, that the origins of Dan, Alice, Larry and Anna's relationships are no more random than countless others, whether the man who marries the work colleague who happened to be assigned the desk next to his, or the woman who leaves her husband for the stranger who happened to be at the same Christmas party.

'Everything that happens in the play is a fluke,' says Marber, and *Closer* expresses his sense of the immense power chance has in all our lives: 'Dan's life was changed by an accident, literally and metaphorically. When he says in the internet scene "Desire like the world is an accident", that's another key line for this play.'

London

It's a play set in a city that I know and live and work in. I wanted it to have the feel of London, was writing it for a London theatre, the National, and never even thought about it being anywhere else. (Patrick Marber)

The London of *Closer* has strong autobiographical connections for Patrick Marber. When he was writing and staging the play, he lived in a flat situated around the corner from Postman's Park, and Alice's early morning walk takes in landmarks that Marber had passed many times while exercising his dog, who, he notes, 'was herself rescued in odd circumstances, but that's another story'. Above and beyond this personal connection, his use of London is simultaneously central and incidental to the play.

Thematically, the changing face of the capital in the mid-1990s preoccupied Marber, as he explained to Nicholas Wright in a Platform Talk at the Cottesloe in May 1997, a week after *Closer* had opened. 'There are a lot of deceptions in the play. The characters constantly lie to each other, deceive each other,' he said. 'I wanted the backdrop, the city itself, to be in some way as deceptive as the characters, so that the London of the play is not everything it seems.' This image of an older, rougher London transformed by 1990s money builds steadily through the play.

Anna's studio has a hidden past:

> **Dan**   What was this building?
>
> **Anna**   A refuge for fallen women. (p. 15)

(by the end, will she view it as a refuge for a twice-abandoned woman?)

Larry recalls that the lapdance club where he meets Alice once looked very different:

> **Larry**   I used to come here twenty years ago . . . it was a punk club . . . the stage was . . .
> *He can't remember, he gives up.* (p. 63)

The filth and fury of punk have given way to mirrors and silicone implants; the club hides its former identity just as the strippers hide theirs. While lapdancing clubs have sprung up all over London since *Closer* opened, in 1997 Marber's use of the club seemed absolutely new, even prescient. 'I'd visited a lapdancing club in Atlanta in 1996, when *Dealer's Choice* was playing in the Olympic Arts Festival, but they didn't have lapdancing clubs in London until at least a year after the play opened. So, as with the internet scene, it contributed to the play feeling very current. I was talking about things that hadn't really happened yet.'

Larry's distaste for the modernising of the punk club is matched by his response to the artificial 'retro' décor of the restaurant where he meets Anna in the following scene: 'The centre of London's a theme park' (Larry, p. 75). A theme park tries to offer all things to all people and none of its zones is real, so to Larry the city itself has no true identity. Meanwhile, there are so many more London sites ripe for redevelopment that Anna can make her latest photographic project a study of derelict buildings (p. 87), while the museum setting of Scene Nine leaves us to think of the lost London now commemorated only through artefacts and manufactured exhibits.

'I was trying to get at the idea of the city spiralling out of control,' Marber told Nicholas Wright in the National Theatre Platform. 'A London that we think we all know but is constantly changing without any seeming pattern to it, new restaurants springing up, just a new London, very very different from the London of the mid-1980s. As Larry says "Everything is a Version of Something Else".'

The sense of London as a mirror for the characters and their deceptions is perhaps strongest in that line of Larry's, and when audiences file out after learning of the death of Jane Jones/Alice Ayres, they may want to paraphrase him: 'Everyone is a Version of Someone Else – or Someone Else's Desires'.

For the National Theatre production, *Closer*'s roots in the capital were deepened by aspects of the sound design (the distinctive noise of black London taxis as they apply their brakes was played in some of the interludes between scenes) and in the programme, which included photographs by Hugo Glendinning of Blackfriars Bridge, St Bartholomew's Hospital, Smithfield Market and Postman's Park.

In performance, however, London is inevitably a city of the audience's imagination – the frame for Marber's portrait of four contemporary urban lives, and that portrait would be almost as effective if framed within another city landscape with large newspaper offices, hospitals, zoo, art galleries, strip clubs, restaurants and airport. 'In my imagining, the play is absolutely set in London,' says Marber, 'but you could just as easily set it in New York or Paris. The story could have happened in any other big city in the world, and having seen it all over the world it appears to be set wherever the play is being staged, whether Paris, or Amsterdam, or Sydney or Berlin. They either keep the references to Smithfield or Blackfriars or change them to "the meat market" or "the bridge".'

In *Closer*, the scale of the setting is nonetheless vitally important: the city as a place of deception and, especially for someone with Larry's roving eye, of limitless sexual possibilities, which give you licence to be selfish with each new partner. As Anna knows to her cost, in a metropolis, 'there's always someone younger' for her first husband or Larry to pursue. Genuine one-to-one intimacy seems more remote than in a village of a few hundred.

Marber remarks: 'Certainly, *Closer* doesn't mean the same if set in a small town and they were bumping into each other in the local store and the Aquarium is in a little local zoo. The London-ness of the play matters to me probably more than it matters to anybody else. What matters most is the sense that surrounding these four people are eight million others. That is important to the play.'

In the theatre, we willingly accept that Larry, Dan, Alice and Anna are the only four inhabitants of this version of the capital. But when this imagined London is replaced by real photographed locations in the film version, and the characters are surrounded by silent extras – visitors to the County Hall Aquarium, art gallery guests, restaurant diners and so on – the story's heightened mood becomes more obviously artificial.

This is a potential problem when any theatrical chamber-piece is 'opened out' for the screen; but the larger the actual location used on film, the more striking it seems when only four characters speak and interact – and this was an issue that Marber says he and Mike Nichols had discussed very early in the adaptation process: 'I was perfectly happy to write incidental characters and have other people speaking. I was prepared to write a scene for Harry Masters, and Anna could've had an assistant and we could've met some of Larry's work colleagues and there could have been a scene for Alice in her dressing room with the other strippers. But Mike said no, that he liked the way the four of them were in their bubble, in the city. That's one of the things I really like about the film.'

So while the film inevitably loses the allusive mood of London in the stage production, through the necessity of showing real locations, Marber believes that Nichols retained some of that heightened quality by permitting only the four characters to speak: 'If you're going to shoot in London you're going to see red buses and stuff. Mike wanted to keep the poetry of the play and the way he did that was isolating the actors within the real city.'

Minor characters

The intense focus on the four leads rarely wavers, and the bare minimum of information about their relations and colleagues that Marber supplies is always used to emphasise or counterpoint the ups and downs of the main quartet.

Dan's mother

After Dan talks about her death in Scene One, Marber has Larry 'resurrect' her in Scene Ten in 'one of the cruellest, most vicious lines in the play':

> **Larry** She tells me you wake in the night, crying for your dead mother.
> *You mummy's boy.* (p. 94)

Larry uses Dan's mother to humiliate Dan and reinforce his own alpha-male status.

Harry Masters

Dan's editor on the obits desk is gay and, according to Alice, hopelessly in love with Dan, who, though he cannot reciprocate, has nonetheless forged a very close bond with Harry, who becomes a kind of surrogate father. Dan seems barely to care about his real father's death, and yet, after losing Anna, spends a week by the dying Harry's hospital bedside. However unhappy the various couplings make the characters, Harry stands silently in the background (and tantalisingly just out of the audience's view at the gallery in Scene Five) as an illustration of the lonely, unfulfilled single life.

Graham

Dan's colleague's most important contribution is his daily catchphrase, 'Who's on the slab?' This works as comedy in the first scene, when it makes Alice chortle, then comes back to haunt Dan in the last, after he learns of her death:

Dan   Graham said, 'Who's on the slab?'
I went out to the fire escape and just . . . cried like a baby.
(p. 113)

Anna's and Larry's parents
At the exhibition in Scene Five, they are used to underline
the class gap between their respective children. Larry's
parents, especially the cab-driver father proud that his
doctor son is dating a photographer, are there as
independent witnesses to how lucky he is to have found such
a high-class woman. Anna's father and stepmother (whose
presence indicates that there is a death or a broken marriage
in her father's past as well as in her own) highlight Larry's
anxiety that Anna may think he's an 'oik': 'So they didn't
think I was "beneath you?"' (p. 47).

Polly
Polly is a young, pretty nurse who enters the background at
the end of the play to show us that Larry has reverted to
type.

Ruth
The two brief references to Dan's girlfriend in Scenes One
and Nine plant seeds that bear fruit in Scene Twelve. We
know in One that Ruth is a linguist and learn from Alice in
Nine that she 'went to pieces when he [Dan] left her' (p. 90).
In Twelve, Marber reveals that Ruth has found the things
that have eluded or been avoided by the principals:
successful marriage and children.

Dan   I bumped into *Ruth*.
She's married. One kid, another on the way.
She married . . . a Spanish *poet*.
He grimaces.
She translated his work and fell in love with him.
Fell in love with a collection of poems.
They were called . . . '*Solitude*'. (p. 114)

These lines and Dan's grimace overflow with regret ('Could it have been me as Ruth's husband, or Alice's?' he's thinking. 'And if I'd married Alice she'd be alive'), incomprehension ('How do some people manage the marriage and kids thing?') and, perhaps, the hope that he might yet find what Ruth has found.

This concluding reference to an unseen happy couple is a beautifully bittersweet grace note, and is particularly interesting because at one stage Marber had planned to make *Closer* a play with six speaking parts: 'There was another couple who were perfectly happy, Jake and Natalie, the contrast couple. I think they knew Dan a bit and one of them might have known Anna. They would just appear now and again, they were sort of the Greek chorus, commenting on the disastrous things that were occurring to their friends, quite happily and smugly sitting in their little flat, perfectly content – and of course they were entirely unnecessary. They would've balanced the criticism that "This is Marber's view of life and love, and can things really be as desperate as this?" They aren't, but one has to be true to the play one's writing. I'm a happily married man now (though I wasn't in 1996–7). I'm a "Jake and Natalie", observing and going "Fucking hell, it's a jungle out there. I'm not there any more, but I have been, and this is what it was like." '

Closer on stage

Closer was written for and first staged at the National Theatre's Cottesloe auditorium, the studio space that, with seating for between three and four hundred people facing a narrow, shallow playing area, is perfectly suited to a series of intimate duologues. If one only reads the play, it is possible to hear the ardour and anger, regret and resentment in the characters' voices, and to visualise from the stage directions how the scenes look. Only in performance can you appreciate the cumulative brilliance of the play's construction, each scene adding another layer to the overall picture, and acting as both foundation and motivation for the next. With the three most theatrical scenes (Three, Six and Eight), reading the text gives one only a fraction of the impact created for a live audience (and it is these three, as discussed on pp. lxxviii–lxxix in '*Closer* on screen', which lose most in translation to the screen).

Cybersex meets Shakespeare

In Scene Three, in the original London production, with the stage divided in half (Dan's desk was stage right and Larry's stage left), the actors were dwarfed by the screen that hung above them, facing the audience, so that everyone in the auditorium could see every line as it was typed, and in effect enter the online chatroom. As the scene builds hilariously to the climax of 'Anna's' orgasm, we must read as well as watch and listen; we are detached observers of Larry's and Dan's reactions to the other's confessions or invitations and can consider ourselves simultaneously in on the joke and its victim: complicit in Dan's manipulation of Larry and yet as unsettled as the doctor, not knowing what 'Anna' will do next.

Dan portrays 'Anna', creating a body and persona to please and tease Larry; Larry's online performance is that of a novice encountering mini-disasters of a very theatrical nature: he is interrupted by 'noises off' (the phone rings); he fluffs his lines (misunderstanding 'Y' as 'Why?' not 'Yes'; mistyping 9£ instead of 9″ when revealing the size of his penis); he thinks his fellow actor may have missed her cue or left the stage entirely ('ANNA? WHERE RU?'). Marber notes: 'This all made sense in 1997, in a world where so many people weren't yet online. Larry is an internet novice, and so were more than half the audience.'

Marber provides a scene of precisely orchestrated yet apparently impromptu performance. This is a playlet-within-the-play, which uses a special form of language even terser and more direct than Marber's writing for the other scenes: the webspeak designed to save time and effort by mostly dispensing with punctuation, capitals and conventional spelling, in this case to speed up the rush towards a sexual hook-up.

In rehearsal, the first attempts at the scene, with actors typing words on to keyboards linked to the display screen, lasted forty minutes. A special software program was developed by Paul Groothius of the National Theatre's sound department so that as soon as an actor began to type, one of the stage management team hit a key and the program instantly ran out the next line of dialogue. This reduced the scene's running time to around six minutes. At each performance, the actors therefore conducted the rhythm of the cues, but the lines appeared at preordained speed. Because different members of the audience read the typing at different speeds, the impact of each line rippled unevenly across the auditorium. The actors could draw out the pause between one typed answer and the next question to allow prolonged laughter to subside, or curtail a pause in which the audience responded less enthusiastically.

Wildly funny and uncomfortably revealing about Dan's and Larry's thoughts on sex (see pp. xliii–xlv), the scene is also the set-up for the Aquarium scene, when Marber delivers that special thrill of our being 'in' on a joke from which the on-stage characters are excluded. What's so striking about this sequence is that while Scene Three is utterly modern, made possible by 1990s technology, it is a variation of a device used by Shakespeare almost four hundred years earlier in *Twelfth Night*. Dan's assumption of Anna's identity is a virtual reworking of Viola's disguise as the page-boy Cesario. The trick played by Dan on Larry is the same as that played in *Twelfth Night* by Maria and Sir Toby Belch on Malvolio, the arrogant household steward who has tried to curb Sir Toby's riotous behaviour. In *Closer*, Dan pretends to be 'Anna' online, and tells Larry to wear his doctor's coat so that she'll know he's the man who's come to the Aquarium for sex. In *Twelfth Night*, Maria, the maid, forges her mistress Countess Olivia's handwriting in a letter dropped for Malvolio to find. In it, 'Olivia' declares her love and specifies what clothes he should wear:

> **Malvolio** '. . . She thus advises thee that sighs for thee.
> Remember who commended thy yellow stockings, and wished
> to see thee ever cross-gartered . . .' (*Twelfth Night*, II, v, lines
> 151–4)

Like Larry, Malvolio follows these instructions precisely and
the pay-off comes in Act Three, Scene Four, when Olivia is
baffled by Malvolio's behaviour and outfit. Though Anna
realises at once that Larry is the victim of a practical joke,
Shakespeare prolongs Olivia's and Malvolio's confusion until
Act Five, Scene One, when she is shown the forged letter:

> **Olivia** Alas! Malvolio, this is not my writing,
> Though, I confess, much like the character;
> But, out of question, 'tis Maria's hand. (lines 344–6)

In *Closer*, the equivalent moment is Anna's realisation that
Dan is behind the prank:

> **Larry** Well I was talking to someone.
> **Anna** (*realising*) Pretending to *be* me.
> You were talking to Daniel Woolf.
> **Larry** Who?
> **Anna** He's Alice's boyfriend. She told me yesterday that he
> plays around on the Net. It's <u>*him*</u>. (pp. 32–3)

Marber told *The Times* in March 1998: 'When I conceived
the scene it was between a man and a woman. They were
going to have met on the Internet, and a different woman
was going to turn up who vaguely fitted the description.
Then I realised I was missing a trick and it was an
opportunity to update the Shakespearean idea of a woman
pretending to be a man.'

Shared space and time
Fluidity of time and location are used to even greater effect
in Scenes Six and Eight. In Six the playing area is again
invisibly divided in two, with Alice and Dan stage left and
Anna and Larry's flat stage right. The actors enter and exit
from opposite sides, their movements precisely
choreographed so that as we listen to Dan saying 'I've been

with Anna', Alice can only picture the two of them in bed, but we can see that Anna is still with Dan, sharing the stage, though not the flat. Then when Alice exits to pack and Larry comes on, Marber reverses the effect: the man Larry dismisses as 'our joke' but who is nonetheless going to break up his marriage is in our view, close enough for Larry to step across and beat him in the 'scrap' he had imagined at the gallery in Scene Five – and yet completely out of his reach. It's hard to convey just how devastating these moments were at the Cottesloe: Dan and Anna standing as both co-perpetrator of and silent witness to the destruction of their lover's marriage/long-term relationship.

Marber creates a different, though equally powerful 'split-screen' in Scene Eight by using just one table. As Anna alternates between the two men, the table and chairs of this wall-less restaurant become a perfect metaphor, simultaneously but separately accommodating Anna's lunch with Larry and dinner with Dan, just as she can accommodate both men in her heart and her bed. Marber builds this image through repetition until the audience is ready to accept the most theatrically daring passage, which begins when Anna challenges Dan to ask Larry if she enjoyed the 'mercy fuck' as Larry 'returns to the table with two drinks'. Now all three are on stage, and with Anna alternately addressing *both* men the trick remains utterly believable while verging on the supernatural; it is as though Dan and Larry become the Invisible Man, or spectres whom only Anna can see.

'I think the restaurant scene is the best in the play, the scene I'm proudest of,' says Marber. 'It does everything I wanted the play to do. That moment when they're on stage together and she's in two different time zones always works if clearly staged. And it makes the scene about *her* and what she's just experienced. It shows her torn between two men. That's the meaning of what's happened to her.'

Set design and music
Marber's original visual concept for the play was

significantly different from the eventual Cottesloe design by Vicki Mortimer, who had designed his production of Craig Raine's *'1953'*. 'Because I knew I had this internet scene I was looking for a justification for this big screen to be above the stage,' Marber says. 'My original idea was for each scene to be titled and for there to be one controlling image for each scene, to emphasise that each scene is differently located. So in my draft script the first scene is titled "Accident" and the image on the screen is a hospital exterior; Two is "Portraits", and the image on screen is rooftops, and so on.

'Vicki's design dealt with that differently, in that we had in effect one piece of furniture for each scene. Through having a projection of Postman's Park as part of the design we wanted to suggest that it would all end there, and wanted the gag of Alice's identity being borrowed from one of the memorials always being there, on stage, for anyone who cared to notice it, but no one did until we put a light on to the Alice Ayres plaque at the end.'

In the programme for *Closer* when it transferred to the Lyttelton Theatre, Mortimer explained: 'For the Cottesloe we tried to design the set so that it appeared to grow from the architecture of the theatre itself. The idea was that the events of the play should seem almost to haunt the space, and the shared memories of the events to mark it.'

In the short interludes between each scene the dominant piece of furniture (camera equipment, computer table, lapdance chair, etc.) from the previous scene was moved upstage centre, to the rear of the playing area, so that by the start of Scene Twelve these physical symbols of the whole play were piled up, as though dumped there by the juggernaut carrying the male 'baggage' Anna talks about in Scene Nine. Mortimer explained to Lyn Gardner of the *Guardian* in January 1998: 'I felt it was crucial in the staging to make it clear that there are echoes beyond the given consequences of any scene. The way the furniture is moved to the back of the stage and stays there throughout makes it clear that everyone's regrets, words and actions remain – they are always there.'

Marber says: 'That [furniture pile] was a symbol of baggage and the past and the domino effect and the idea that each scene cannot have happened without the preceding one. And by the end they've all made a big mess of their lives, so here's all this stuff that's been accumulated. There's a line in Oscar Wilde's *The Picture of Dorian Gray* that I've always wanted to use as the title of a play, where a character says that the mind of modern man "is like a bric-a-brac shop, all monsters and dust". *Monsters and Dust* would be a very good title.'

The ambiguity of this symbol – might the furniture be reclaimed, sold off, thrown away, burned? – provides another example of how Marber, as he puts it, is 'always trying to ignite the audience's imagination without telling them what they're seeing. A lot of this comes from Harold Pinter: the ignition of a series of meanings and possibilities about what it is that's being said and seen. I like things to cohere, but to cohere differently for each member of the audience.'

The scene changes were carried out to the accompaniment of Paddy Cunneen's haunting and haunted cello music and a soundtrack of London traffic noise, with distinctive black-taxi brakes to the fore. The sound designer Simon Baker told the *Guardian*: 'It was a question of setting Paddy's music within the London landscape of the play. I went for a generic and quite aggressive sound – lots of taxi brakes, which I think for most people are really the sound of London. I melded that with Paddy's strings. It gives quite a hardcore edge, a sense of the anonymous city.' Marber recalls it: 'We also used the crackle and whine of the internet dial-up noise for Scene Three, which dates us.'

In an article for *Closer*'s Lyttelton programme, Cunneen said: 'Traffic roaring over cello solos somehow helps to keep the music in its place in the play. I was pleased with the way that the music's emotional yearning is buried but not lost in the city soundscape.'

Casting

For Alice, Patrick Marber took a considerable risk by casting Liza Walker, who had never previously acted on stage. But the gamble paid off handsomely: Walker could not do anything other than play the youngest and most impulsive of the four characters on instinct, rather than falling back on techniques honed through years of stage experience; she seemed as fresh and 'disarming' to audiences as to Dan.

This Alice was slim, dark-haired, pale and fine-featured. Matt Wolf in *Variety* noted how her 'waiflike appearance co-exists with the apparently steely child-woman who moves between Dan and Larry', and Marber has acknowledged that this duality in the character emerged partly in response to Walker's approach in rehearsals.

With an occasionally rough, working-class edge to her voice, Walker stood in effectively stark contrast, in age, voice and looks, to the home-counties tones and more voluptuous figure of Sally Dexter's Anna: 'Dexter is as Rubensian as Walker is mysterious and gaunt,' wrote Matt Wolf. Dexter, a very experienced stage actress who had taken part in some of the *Closer* workshops at the NT Studio, earned a Best Actress nomination at the Olivier Awards for a performance of 'resonant sensuality' (Nick Curtis, *Evening Standard*), which emphasised Anna's increasing weariness at being let down again and again by the men in her life, without sacrificing her wry sense of humour.

Marber had written Larry as a Londoner, but told the NT Platform audience in 1999 that he was happy to ignore this aspect of the character when he realised that the Irishman Ciaran Hinds 'was the best possible actor for the part'. Already in his mid-forties when cast, and looking old enough to be Liza Walker's father, Hinds has a dark, burly and brooding stage presence. His Larry had mature, easygoing charm but, when roused (his fury at Anna in Scene Six, his frustration at Alice's answers in Seven), the result was genuinely intimidating. His superb comic timing helped him fully to exploit what Benedict Nightingale in *The Times* called 'the rueful comedy amid the pain'. (Hinds also played the part on Broadway.)

Nightingale's description of Dan as 'the chilled and chilling journo' neatly sums up Clive Owen's performance, which, quite rightly, made the younger man seem aloof and emotionally inaccessible even when he was declaring his love for Anna or Alice.

Explaining his casting decisions at the National Theatre Platform on *Closer* in 1999, Marber said all four actors were chosen because they were 'a little bit like the characters, understood what the play was about and had been through the mill a bit romantically'. Marber says: 'Looking back, I'd say the chemistry between these four, as people and as actors, was pretty much perfect. I got very lucky. Without their brilliance and patience and the particular qualities they had, individually and collectively, the original production would not have had anything like the impact it did. *Plus* all four were sexy as hell – which sure helps this play take life.'

What the actors said

Sally Dexter, on playing Anna in the NT Studio workshop and the National Theatre production: 'I had had a very painful emotional upheaval in my own life at the time, and it was a cathartic experience to channel those feelings into the play. I was amazed at how honest and fresh Patrick's script was, how modern' (*Evening Standard*, 8 October 1997). In January 1998, she told the *Guardian*: 'This play makes you dig into your soul. When I'm on stage, it is genuinely upsetting. I can't divorce myself from it. It is hugely painful and enjoyable at the same time.'

Liza Walker, on playing Alice in the London production: 'I love the fact that Alice does what she wants and that the play is so real. It doesn't shock just for effect: there's a purpose to it' (*Evening Standard*). Walker told the *Guardian*: 'I understood it immediately: I'd been through relationships like that. I thought it was really courageous because it said all the things that people think but no one has the nerve to say. I think Patrick probably does think that I am Alice. I don't know whether that's a good or a bad thing. I do find it quite difficult to snap out of her.'

Mark Strong, who played Dan in the workshop and then replaced Clive Owen in the part when *Closer* transferred to the 900-seat Lyttelton Theatre, told the *Guardian*: 'I always wondered [at the workshop stage] how the thing was going to stand up when it got to production, because it's a bunch of four people reacting quite cerebrally. There are not obvious theatrical fireworks. It's very lean. In the more intimate Cottesloe, *Closer* opened to silence. I think people felt brutalised. In the bigger Lyttelton they are more dispassionate and distanced, so they can laugh more.'

What the critics said
Extracts from British reviews of the National Theatre production and from US reviews of the Broadway transfer in March 1999:

John Peter, *Sunday Times*: 'This is a dark, compassionate, humane play in which Marber's control cohabits wisely, sadly and in some puzzlement with his tolerance and indignation as a man. He knows that people learn little, if anything, from experience. His writing is lyrical, brutally scabrous and unflinchingly realistic: he knows the language of excitement and despair.'

Charles Spencer, *Daily Telegraph*: 'The f-words and c-words acquire an intensity I don't think it's pretentious to describe as poetic . . . Not the least of this play's accomplishments is that you become desperate to know what is going to happen to its anguished, vulnerable characters next . . . My only complaint is that the play's structure seems a touch too neat for its subject matter . . . I'd be astonished if there's a better new play this year.'

John Gross, *Sunday Telegraph*: 'They put on all kinds of different plays at the National Theatre and last week they gave us a soap opera. A superior soap opera, it is true; but a work which doesn't leave much trace once (so to speak) you

have switched off the set . . . The overall effect is one of
manipulation. You get a frisson from watching the members
of the quartet rend one another, but you can't quite believe
in them. It is all a spectacle.'

Alastair Macaulay, *Financial Times*: 'On the surface, *Closer* is
brisk, urbane, witty, obscene, modern, quotable, slick;
beneath the skin, it is deeply felt, painful, sad, and wise . . .
Marber seems to me to have the most assured sense for
dramatic rhythm of any English playwright to have emerged
since Pinter.'

Michael Billington, *Guardian*: 'Marber takes no sides or
prisoners in this candid, scathing, very modern view of the
sex war. At different times, he suggests, we are all predators
and victims . . . What lingers is Marber's sense that,
however much they couple or fraternise, men and women
remain forever trapped inside their own skins.'

Nick Curtis, *Evening Standard*: 'This is pessimistic stuff but
Closer is rarely sombre. The script is studded with dry,
understated wit and moments of rare inspiration.'

Sheridan Morley, *Spectator*: 'This is *Private Lives* for the late
nineties, a story of four people who can live neither together
nor apart but whose electric attraction to each other finally
burns all of them out in a shock ending which has in fact
been very carefully prepared if only we could have seen it
coming. Like Coward, but precious few others, Marber has
a remarkable talent for making us fall in love with appalling
people, and here their fatal attraction is what drives the play
across the borders of comedy and tragedy.'

Charles Isherwood, *Daily Variety*: '*Closer* is both bruising and
beautiful, shatteringly funny and devastatingly sad. It feels
ripped from the heart . . . and it leaves a lasting scar there
. . . Have the tortured dynamics of love and need ever been
laid bare as honestly onstage as they are here? . . . The
play's sad message is that the truth of the heart is ever-
changing, and tainted by other equally liquid emotions:

jealousy, pride, selfishness, lust. Love's a paltry, unreliable, painful thing, Marber's bleakly beautiful play tells us – how grim and how funny, then, that it is all we have to ward off the terrors of life and death.'

David Patrick Stearns, *USA Today*: 'No other recent play so beautifully captures the jittery, life-imitates-MTV superficiality of modern urban existence. The stranger on the street may change your life, but these relationships are like recreational drugs, fun for a while but invitations to alienation.'

Fintan O'Toole, *Daily News*: 'Each of the actors creates a completely convincing character . . . But the script gives none of them the room to make those characters change and grow before our eyes; Marber is too intent on easy pessimism to allow that to happen. In the end, *Closer* is too satisfied with its own dark vision to risk any real emotion. That makes it ultimately as cold and self-absorbed as its characters.'

Linda Winer, *Newsday*: 'What a nasty bit of work is *Closer* – nasty, dirty-talking, loveless and, oh, yes, riveting erotic theatre. It also happens to be a lot less meaningful or important than its author-director Patrick Marber and its wheelbarrows of recent London awards would have us believe. Chances are, however, audiences will be too seduced – or, in sensitive cases, bludgeoned – by its hard-edged sexual politics and electrifying actors to notice the emptiness, until the darkly funny, aggressively unromantic comedy is over.'

Ben Brantley, *New York Times*: 'Despite the many excoriating exchanges among the characters, you only fitfully believe in their capacity to be hurt, and for the most part you don't care whether they are or not. *Closer* is all too close to Alice's description of Anna's portraits: "a bunch of sad strangers photographed beautifully".'

Closer on screen

Casting

When the film of *Closer* was in pre-production the cast had two Englishmen, Jude Law as Dan and Clive Owen as Larry, the American Natalie Portman as Alice and the Australian Cate Blanchett, who had signed to play Anna, probably as an Englishwoman. But Blanchett had to withdraw in September 2003 when she became pregnant with her second child. When Nichols wanted to approach Julia Roberts as her replacement and asked Marber 'How do you feel about an American as Anna?', the writer was very comfortable with the prospect, largely because of his experience with the Broadway production, when the American Polly Draper took over from the English Natasha Richardson midway through the six-month run. 'I asked Polly to do it with an American accent and wrote extra material for her to explain why she was working in London; to show, for example, that her first husband was English. A lot of that survived into the film for Julia Roberts. So I'd heard Anna as American and already knew it worked.'

He was equally comfortable with Portman as an American Alice, partly because of the built-in element of the character having travelled and worked as a stripper in the US, and partly because he had auditioned many American actresses for the role on Broadway (even though it eventually went to the English Anna Friel). 'I'd often heard Alice with an American accent in those auditions, so knew that it worked fine. I felt Dan and Larry couldn't be American. But always knew that Anna and Alice could be, because the play isn't about necessarily English people, it's about the personality and activity and actions of these people. One of the reasons it gets done everywhere is that nationality is not the central element.'

Roberts's global status as the most bankable Hollywood actress of her generation, and Portman's lesser, though still considerable international fame through her role as Padmé in all three *Star Wars* prequels, unquestionably made *Closer* a much more marketable film at US and international box-offices than it might have been with lesser-known English actresses in the roles (or indeed with Blanchett). It took more than $115 million worldwide – an exceptionally high figure for an adult-themed contemporary drama not aimed at a mainstream audience, as Marber told the trade newspaper *Variety* in January 2005: 'We knew we were making a film that had a lot of dialogue and long scenes and that it wouldn't appeal to everyone.'

Clive Owen, who had played Dan at the National Theatre, stepped comfortably into the role of Larry. On screen he had specialised in sardonic charmers with rough-diamond sex appeal, notably in his breakthrough appearance as the wide-boy title character in two series of the TV crime drama *Chancer* (1990–1), as the title character in the London-set film thriller *Croupier* (1998) and as an insolent valet in *Gosford Park* (2001). All of these characters might be labelled, like Larry, as a 'clinical observer of the human carnival' and because the default setting for Owen's line readings is ironic detachment, he has just the right tone for Larry's observations on everything from sex to urban redevelopment to skin disease.

Owen's height and heavy build made the physical gap between him and Natalie Portman's petite, girlish Alice as great as the gulf in the characters' ages. Portman was twenty-two when the film was shot, but looks several years younger, giving the impression that she simply cannot have been around long enough to have experienced as much as the stage Alices of more mature-looking actresses such as Liza Walker in London or Anna Friel on Broadway. Though this aspect makes Portman's Alice seem preternaturally wise and certain about the ways of love and sex, she brings off more convincingly the contrast between Alice's heartbreaking vulnerability (particularly when Dan leaves her) and her total physical assurance (the strip club scene) – the duality that, in Larry's crude terms, makes it easy to understand why men are equally keen to father her and fuck her.

With Jude Law, even in spectacles and a dowdy grey raincoat, the actor's stunning good looks are at odds with the nerdish, awkward Dan of the opening scene (Marber even gives Larry a new line for the screenplay's gallery scene, telling Anna that Dan is 'very pretty'). The selfish, vain lover that Dan becomes is much more in Law's line, drawn from the same stock as his Bosie in *Wilde* (1997), Errol Flynn in *The Aviator* or the title character in *Alfie* (both 2004).

Julia Roberts had never played such a complex, mature role as Anna. Ever since she became a superstar in *Pretty Woman* (1990), Hollywood has consistently exploited her vivacity, thousand-watt smile and explosive laugh in lightweight comedies (*My Best Friend's Wedding, Runaway Bride*) and thrillers (*The Pelican Brief, Conspiracy Theory*), and even her Oscar-winning performance in *Erin Brockovich* (2000) had a much sunnier disposition than one would expect in a drama about a real-life class action against a water-polluting power company. Roberts therefore excels as Anna not only because Nichols's direction and Marber's script allow her to explore the more restrained, introverted end of her acting range, but also because Anna plays against audience expectations of Roberts the wisecracking, ultra-confident leading lady. Anyone familiar with Roberts's most popular roles is taken aback to see her in such comparatively downbeat, unsympathetic light, as a divorcee-turned-home-wrecking adulteress; in particular, the forensic sexual detail of Anna's confrontation with Larry in their flat is all the more shocking because audiences had never previously heard her devliver such explicit dialogue.

Structure and imagery
Though line-by-line comparison between Marber's play and screenplay reveals many small changes and cuts to the dialogue (in total, about thirty per cent of the lines are missing), the overall structure of both is the same, with two notable omissions and one major addition: Scenes Nine and Twelve are missing and there is a new final sequence. For a ninety-minute Hollywood film made in 2004 to contain only a dozen scenes/sequences, all lasting between five and eleven minutes, is extremely rare – and shows how

determined Marber and Nichols were to avoid the
traditional approach to filming plays: namely to take long
stage scenes set in one room and break them up into
sequences of shorter scenes set in several locations. The one
occasion where they adopt this conventional tactic is at the
start of the film.

It opens with Dan and Alice walking towards one another
along a crowded London street, accompanied on the
soundtrack by the Damien Rice love song 'The Blower's
Daughter', with its chorus of 'I can't take my eyes off of
you'. Their eyes meet from opposite sides of the street. We
see the accident and its immediate aftermath, the taxi ride,
and then their conversation in a hospital Accident and
Emergency waiting room filled with extras. They do not
meet Larry, because, says Marber, whereas in a play an
audience can accept lots of coincidences, in the more literal
medium of film 'there is such a huge coincidence for people
to take with the Aquarium, and we felt one was enough'.
The flirting continues as Dan gives her a running
commentary on their walk through London, pointing out 'a
red bus . . . policemen, or "bobbies" ', and their visit to
Postman's Park, where Dan talks about the aftermath of his
mother's death and we see Alice looking intently at one
particular memorial (though we don't see which one). They
talk while seated on the top deck of a bus to Dan's office
and, finally, Alice reveals her name on the concourse in
front of the newspaper building.

Where Scene One of the play offered only dialogue,
Nichols's energetic and varied opening sequence hooks and
reels us into the story and the setting with a mixture of
establishing incident and spectacle (the London locations)
and movement (walking, taxi and bus journey) that always
serves, rather than obscures the dialogue. The director
hopes that after this we'll be in settled and attentive mood,
primed to absorb the more claustrophobic and static scenes
that follow.

From this point onwards, there are only a handful of
moments when Nichols moves the focus away from the
original stage setting: the last third of the Aquarium scene

places Larry and Anna outdoors on the Embankment. The first exchange between Dan and Alice from Scene Five (up to Alice: 'Why won't you let me love you?') is set in their small, cosy flat, as Dan shaves and Alice gets ready to finish dressing (this is a superb addition to the play, giving us a preparatory, and slightly ominous, glimpse of the couple's domestic life just a few minutes before we see them together again at the flat in the break-up scene). We see Dan putting Alice into a taxi outside the gallery before going back inside to talk to Anna. Nichols also shows Larry arriving in a taxi at his and Anna's vast loft apartment. Dan is shown briefly in the street outside Larry's surgery and in the waiting room before he goes into the consulting room, and in the airport hotel corridor and lift when he aborts his trip to buy cigarettes at the terminal.

Marber: 'I think Mike wanted to show a bit of London in that opening sequence, and we also felt that to start the film completely static [as in the play] could kill it. We wanted it to have a bit of scale at the beginning and then start closing in on the characters. When I wrote the screenplay I was quite happy to break up other scenes into smaller pieces but Mike always wanted to preserve the structure of the play and have four speaking roles only. That was a given. Very brave of him, I think. He was never afraid of it being "too theatrical".'

For the next eighty minutes, therefore, Nichols does his best to replicate the intimacy and intensity of the play. Rather than cutting between a number of angles, he mostly uses just one camera to cover each scene, favours long takes and tight, emotionally revealing close-ups. As the director of photography Stephen Goldblatt noted in *Variety* in January 2005: 'We concentrated on bringing the audience into intimate contact with the four main characters, and not distracting them from the dialogue.'

On many occasions, Nichols, Goldblatt and the production designer Tim Hatley find visual equivalents for *Closer*'s examination of the slippery nature of identity: the reflections of faces in mirrors in Dan's flat, the strip club, the airport hotel, in Anna's camera lenses, computer screens or in the glass walls of the Aquarium tanks; the translucent walls of the private room in the strip club. The cold, bleak dialogues are set against a cold, grey palette; black is a predominant colour in the principals' costumes.

Editing and viewpoints

In the tone and narrative techniques of the scenes set in the hospital, photography studio, gallery, strip club, consulting room and the hotel, there is little difference between the play and the film. Stage scenes such as these, involving a single location and timeframe, are the most straightforward to translate to the screen. But there are three scenes (Three, Six and Eight) where the differences in presentation between play and film are so striking that they are worth examining in detail.

On stage in the cybersex scene, with no physical barriers between the two rooms, Marber could allow each audience member to switch their attention between Dan, Larry and the giant computer screen, but all three elements formed a unified stage picture. On film, to retain the comic and shock effects of the audience reading the dialogue as it's typed, Nichols has to show each man's screen separately. And, having decided not to show both men at their keyboards in a split-screen variation on the familiar cinematic trick of simultaneously showing the speakers at both ends of a telephone conversation, he also needs to cut between Dan and Larry. So instead of the unified stage picture we have four complementary and yet competitive elements – Dan, Larry and their respective computers – each 'fighting' for screen time. We cut between Dan's typing, the scrolling text on the computer screens and Larry's reaction, and vice versa, but are denied the supreme pleasure of watching all three at once.

If the stage and film versions of the internet scene illustrate the difference between theatre's and cinema's use of space and control of audience perspective, then the film's treatment of Scenes Six and Eight shows how difficult it is for cinema to match theatre's fluidity of time and location.

As discussed on pp. lxiv–lxv, on stage there are no physical or temporal boundaries dividing Larry and Anna's break-up row from Dan and Alice's in Scene Six; in the film, Nichols can only seek to replicate the sense of overlapping, mirrored action by cutting back and forth between the two apartments. So Scene Six becomes a sequence: Dan and Alice, then Larry and Anna, then back to see Alice leaving, then back to Larry and Anna; Dan alone; Larry and Anna. The editing links the two events as closely as it can, but the result is nowhere near as affecting as when, alternately, Anna and Dan remain in the audience's view as both cause of and silent witness to the separations.

The restaurant scene in the play becomes a sequence divided between five locations: the restaurant at the National Portrait Gallery where Anna and Larry meet for their abortive lunch, the circle bar, gentlemen's toilet and balcony at the Theatre Royal, Drury Lane (doubling for the opera house where Anna and Dan meet), and Larry's consulting room, where we see the couple dressing after sex. It begins with Larry's arrival and then, when he goes to the bar for drinks, cuts to Anna's late arrival at the opera, where she has to meet Dan in the bar as they've missed the start of the first act. Once the dialogue has established that Anna's two meetings are set on the same day, the editing reinforces Marber's original intention to make this very much Anna's scene; the cutaway flashbacks to her afternoon with Larry, prompted by Dan's questions and angry responses to her revelations, make us feel as though she is replaying the afternoon in her head.

'It's true that in the film you don't get that split-screen effect in those scenes,' Marber concedes, 'but what you gain is the close-up, and a different rhythm, and you see things you could never see on stage. The whole film for me is summed up in the scene in the restaurant – the way that Julia Roberts reacts to Larry's big speech, all the film is contained in her eyes for me, in that scene. All the curdled, strange desire, you'd never get that on the stage. Her performance in that scene is one of the highlights of the film for me.'

There are other, equally telling close-ups, such as the fleeting shot of Portman's face just after Alice has entered Anna's studio, which tells us instantly that she *knows* something's going on between Anna and Dan – a moment echoed by the close-up on Owen when Larry has been 'spying' on Anna and Dan at the gallery.

In between the break-up and opera/restaurant sequences, comes the one scene substantially more erotic and unsettling on film than on stage: Larry's encounter with Alice in the club. Here, design, sound, music, cinematography and acting combine to give the scene a voyeuristic charge more potent than in the theatre. Tim Hatley built a private room with translucent walls, so that Larry and Alice are secluded without our losing sight of the activity in the background. Nichols's choice of music adds another layer. The scene begins with the percussive violence and verbal misogyny of the Prodigy's 'Smack My Bitch Up' playing in the background, followed by The Smiths' 'How Soon is Now?', with lyrics that might have been written for the emotional needs and immediate predicaments of both Alice and Larry, as Morrissey sings of the universal human need for love and a futile visit to a nightclub in search of a lover.

Above all, it's the camerawork and editing that make every cinemagoer as much of a voyeur as Larry: we are given no choice but to stare at Natalie Portman's near-naked body. The close-ups bring us as close to her as Clive Owen, as her breasts, legs and bottom fill the screen. 'The film certainly adds something to that scene,' says Marber, 'and gives it some kind of sleaze that is harder to achieve on stage.'

The three most significant changes come in the final quarter of the film. The film excludes Scene Nine, at the museum. The absence of the intense confrontation between Anna and Alice after Larry has left them alone at the museum leaves their on-screen relationship underdeveloped compared to the stage version, and, for Anna's character journey, removes a crucial bridge between her having sex with Larry at the consulting room and going back to him. A slightly altered line in the most confessional moment of the screen version of the hotel scene partially compensates for the absence of Scene Nine:

> **Alice** Larry fucked me all night. I enjoyed it. I came. Now go.

Dan believes that they merely had a one-night stand, not a relationship of several months, so the formal symmetry of the play – four characters become four couples for significant periods of time – has been sacrificed.

'I did write a version of Scene Nine in the screenplay,' explains Marber, 'and would say Mike's decision to omit it was the one area where we had any level of disagreement. It was completely amiable, but he said "Look, this scene is not plot-necessary, we can make the film work without this scene." My argument was "No, it isn't plot-necessary but it probably is character-necessary." I think that the film would've been too long with it in, but I slightly mourn its loss, mainly because I'd have liked to have seen Julia and Natalie do it, because they'd have done it really well. Mike was much more interested in the Larry story and the Alice story in the second half of the film, and I think he wanted to focus more on that. His conception of the thing was that in the first half it's all about Dan and Anna and in the second half Larry and Alice.'

The screen versions of Scenes Ten and Eleven differ little from the play. When Dan slaps Alice across the face in the hotel room we fade into a closing sequence that is perhaps the most cinematic in the film; after so much talk, Nichols and Marber tie up all the loose ends with just four words of dialogue, rather than eleven pages of it in the play. To a reprise of Damien Rice singing 'The Blower's Daughter', we see Anna awake in bed alongside Larry, who is contentedly asleep. She disentangles her hand from his, turns out the light and turns on her side, and the final close-up of Roberts's face shows a woman far from certain that this apparently blissful domesticity will endure. We cut to Alice arriving at the immigration desk of a New York airport, handing her passport to an immigration officer. We see a close-up of her name as Jane Jones, and the officer (played by Colin Stinton from Marber's stage production of *The Old Neighborhood*) says: 'Welcome back, Miss Jones.' Cut to Dan in London, wearing the same spectacles, grey raincoat and suit from the opening scene, walking into Postman's Park and stopping, stunned, in front of one of the commemorative plaques: cut to a close-up reveal of the Alice Ayres text. Finally, Portman walks in slow motion up Broadway towards the camera, looking sexier than ever, turning every male passer-by's head, en route to a future of endless possibilities; whereas in the play she has no future. (Though conspiracy theorists on the internet have noticed that she walks through a 'Stop' sign and conjecture that she's walking to her death as in the play.)

The bittersweet nature of the ending is emphatically underscored by Rice's song, in which a lover who in this context might be Dan, looks back on a broken relationship. Over and over in the first two choruses he sings 'I can't take my eyes off of you'; then, in the third chorus: 'I can't take my mind off of you'. The final, deeply ironic line – ''Til I find somebody new' – sums up in five words *Closer*'s preoccupation with the intensity and fickleness of love.

Of this altered ending, Marber says: 'Some people when interviewing me about the film said, "How do you feel about this betrayal of what you wrote?" It just so isn't like that. Mike and I came up with that scene together. I think that to be faithful to something, you can be faithful to the spirit without being faithful to the action of it. In the end Mike's final vision was "Oh, I don't want to kill Alice". It's a movie and I love that, the freedom of it.'

Of Alice's survival, Marber says: 'I know that objectively it is a big difference because in the play she dies and in the film she survives, but I feel it's the same ending, because for me the shape of the play is four strangers meet, fall in love, fall out of love and go their separate ways. In the play one of them happens to die but that for me isn't the meaning of the play, the meaning of the play is that they're all alone in the end. We had shot the Postman's Park ending, and we looked at Dan making a big long speech and Anna and Larry are apart and Alice is no longer alive and we looked at it and went, "Nah, this is no good, not working." It was no fun, so we came up with a whole different way of ending the film.'

He argues that this problem has less to do with the need for even an emotionally bleak Hollywood film to have an at least partially upbeat ending than the intrinsic difference between stage and screen: that Scene Twelve works beautifully on stage as a diminuendo, a dying fall, whereas on film it jarred and 'felt like a scene in a play'. Julia Roberts was called back to London for a half-day's work in which the scene of her and Owen in bed was filmed, and even though Larry and Anna are together at the end of the film, Marber argues that it finishes 'one beat before the play: we're between Scenes Eleven and Twelve. The look on Anna's face tells us that she knows the relationship is going to end. It's provisional and they probably won't last, but we don't know that; they might muddle through, they might not.'

Time on screen
Marber feels that *Closer* was 'amazingly' edited by John Bloom and Antonia Van Drimmelen, especially in the transitions from one scene to the next, as months evaporate in seconds – though, as on stage, the passage of time only emerges organically, through the dialogue. 'We debated whether we should fade to black and give you a caption saying "A month later", or whatever, but decided not to because we wanted to make a film where the audience have to work it out. It was a key decision as to what kind of film we were making. Were we making a film where we were going to do our best to respect the audience and assume they were intelligent beings who would work it out, or were we going to feed them the information? It'd be an easier film to get hold of if we told you it's a day later, a year later, a month later, the audience would feel more comfortable. But Mike didn't want the audience to feel entirely

comfortable. It's an unnerving film, just as *Carnal Knowledge* is' (see below).

Nichols and his editors also enhance the retrospective dialogue of the hotel scene with two flashbacks that accompany the characters' spoken recollections of Dan's visit to the club (shots of Alice pole-dancing in bra and panties, and Dan's shocked reaction), and the cab journey after her road accident (the kiss on the forehead and his telling the cabbie 'She's mine'). The visual and spoken references back to the start of the story help us subconsciously to be prepared for its imminent conclusion.

Further viewing

'Carnal Knowledge' (1971)
Reviewing Mike Nichols's film of *Closer* in *Variety*, Todd McCarthy, found it 'intriguing as a companion piece to the director's early-career studies of the sexual battleground, *Who's Afraid of Virginia Woolf?* and especially *Carnal Knowledge*'. Indeed, when Nichols first met Marber to discuss *Closer* he asked the playwright if he had been influenced by *Carnal Knowledge*. 'I hadn't seen it,' says Marber, 'but I subsequently saw the film and could understand why Mike thought I had. It's a very tough four-hander about misogyny – a very odd, interesting, nasty film that definitely informs *sex, lies and videotape*.'

The similarities between *Closer, sex, lies and videotape* and *Carnal Knowledge* are arresting. All three were deemed to have captured a particular moment in the ongoing battle of the sexes, *Carnal Knowledge* examining the emotional consequences of the 1960s sexual revolution before the reflections of Soderbergh and Marber on, respectively, the 1980s and 1990s. In *Carnal Knowledge* we have another attractive urban quartet, two men and two women, this time a doctor, an accountant, a would-be-lawyer turned home-maker and a model. There is a great deal of sex and sex talk, but precious little warmth or love, and the dominant themes of Jules Feiffer's terse, acidic screenplay resemble

Marber's: the selfishness and transience of sexual desire and the seemingly irreconcilable differences between male and female attitudes to sex and love.

Though broken up into more than twenty scenes, *Carnal Knowledge* is structured like a three-act play and, as with *sex, lies and videotape*, one could imagine it translated effectively to the stage.

Feiffer tells the story of best friends and college room-mates Sandy (Art Garfunkel) and Jonathan (Jack Nicholson), whom we first meet in the late 1950s as freshmen. Sandy begins dating the beautiful Susan (Candice Bergen), a student at a neighbouring college. Behind his friend's back, Jonathan starts seeing Susan, eventually losing his virginity by taking hers. Jonathan's obsession with women as sexual objects and inability to give and receive love is immediately apparent, and he fiercely resents the emotional intimacy that Susan shares with Sandy. He ends the relationship without revealing the betrayal, and, with the sexes reversed, the dynamic here is echoed in *Closer*. Susan wants to protect the 'vulnerable' and 'helpless' Sandy; Dan holds back from revealing his affair with Anna and wounding Alice.

The second 'act' begins about ten years later in New York City, with Sandy, now a qualified doctor, married to Susan, with two children and a large, comfortable home. Jonathan, now a successful, promiscuous accountant, begins a relationship with the model Bobbie (Ann-Margaret) that begins in delirious sexual frenzy but starts to decline as soon as Bobbie moves into his bachelor pad. After giving up modelling at Jonathan's instigation, she loses all purpose, becoming virtually housebound and sleeping through the day. When she tells Jonathan that if he won't marry her she'll leave him, he calls her a 'ball-busting, castrating, son of a cunt bitch!', and she takes an overdose of sleeping pills.

The brief final act takes place another ten years later. Sandy is now in a relationship with an eighteen-year-old, Jennifer, and may finally have found love. Jonathan, now forty, has divorced Bobbie, and moans about the alimony payments to ex-wife and daughter. His misogyny has deepened so far that it is affecting his sexual potency, and the devastating final scene reveals that this once rampant lothario can only achieve an erection with a prostitute, Louise (Rita Moreno), who has to stimulate him with a scripted rant against the women who fail to realise 'that the purest form of love is of a man who denies himself to her . . . because he has no need for any woman'. Even *Closer*'s self-styled caveman might blanch at that, yet Jonathan's plight can be viewed as a salutary warning of where Larry's relentless objectification of women (the online chatroom, the New York hooker, the strip club, treating Anna as his whore) might lead him ten years down the line.

'Your Friends & Neighbors' (1998)

The American writer-director Neil LaBute's second feature film was released less than eighteen months after *Closer*'s London stage premiere, and repays study as a contemporary US counterpart to the play. It lacks *Closer*'s humour but shares its sexually explicit language and formal symmetry, as a group of six attractive urban professionals in their thirties (two couples, a single man and a single woman) swap partners in a far-from-merry-go-round of cold, unfulfilling marital and extra-marital sex.

To an even greater extent than Marber, LaBute is a disciple of David Mamet, and *Your Friends & Neighbors* apes the structure of *Sexual Perversity in Chicago* (dozens of fairly short scenes, all but a handful involving just two characters). LaBute also takes the misogyny of *Sexual Perversity*'s lothario, Bernard, and pushes it to provocatively unpalatable extremes in the shape of the monstrous Cary (the smouldering Jason Patric), a promiscuous doctor who hones his sexual technique with stopwatch-timed solo thrusting in an empty bed, regards all women as 'cunts' and 'bitches', and says that his best ever fuck was the homosexual gang-rape of a high-school classmate.

Cary is best friends with businessman Barry (Aaron Eckhart), who is suffering impotence with his meek, journalist wife Mary (Amy Brenneman). Barry is also friendly with Jerry (Ben Stiller), a college drama professor co-habiting in a fractious long-term relationship with an advertising copywriter, Terri (Catherine Keener), whose bisexuality emerges when she meets a beautiful art gallery assistant, Cheri (Nastassja Kinski).

In the film's 100 bitter minutes, Terri and Cheri begin an affair; Cheri rebuffs Cary; Mary and Jerry meet for sex in a hotel but Jerry can't perform; Terri rebuffs Cary; Mary leaves Barry, moves in with and falls pregnant by Cary; Terri and Cheri move in together and Jerry takes up with one of his female students; now alone, Barry can no longer even achieve an erection by masturbating. As in *Closer*, the wheels come full circle. There is a sense that despite all the upheaval LaBute's characters remain as dissatisfied as when we first met them, whereas Marber insists that the survivors in *Closer* are 'older and wiser', despite Larry's assertion that nobody changes.

Watching *Your Friends & Neighbors* is an uncomfortable experience because LaBute piles on layers of alienation that make it as hard for us to get our bearings or engage emotionally with his characters as it is for them to connect with each other. The characters' rhyming, identikit first names are used only in the cast list, never in the script; instead, people are only referred to as 'the wife', 'that bitch', 'my best friend' etc. Every scene takes place indoors and although Cary refers to the big city in which the sextet live and work we have no idea of where in America this might be. It's a city even more conducive to coincidental encounters than the London of *Closer*, as the characters keep bumping into one another at the same bookshop and museum. The atmosphere is at its most artificial in the four scenes in which Cheri meets first Terri then Cary, Barry and finally Jerry at the gallery, and each engages her in conversation by asking of a particular exhibit: 'Is this part of a collection?'

Though the characters in both works are equally preoccupied with the comparative quality of sex with different partners, Marber's is a much more balanced portrait, not least because he allows each couple a period of initial happiness that makes their subsequent fallings-out all the more painful. With the fleeting exception of Terri and Cheri, LaBute's couples are miserable or unfulfilled all the time, regardless of who they're with – prompting the critic Peter Matthews, in his *Sight & Sound* review, to suggest that 'LaBute might as well come out and admit he thinks everybody's a clone'.

LaBute's dialogue, like Marber's, is often shocking, yet superficial by comparison. To take just one example, when Cary talks to Terri for the only time in the film and dismisses her as 'a useless cunt', the insult is the product of one-dimensional characterisation; he hardly knows Terri and we've already heard him talk like this to and about other women, so the line is shocking but not sufficiently motivated to be convincing or moving. By contrast, when Larry calls Anna a 'FUCKED-UP SLAG' in *Closer*, the words pour from a wellspring of guilt, anger and loss shared by two intimately connected and by this point familiar characters. With Marber, the shock of language is, in every sense of the word, heartfelt.

Though some viewers find *Closer* a cold, alienating experience, unable to care about four people who speak and act in such a clinical fashion, for many thousands of others the play unflinchingly mirrors episodes from their own lives. There are tales of audience members weeping in their seats at the painful personal memories awakened by, for instance, Alice's uncomprehending grief at Dan's infidelity. The play could never have succeeded on stage in more than a hundred cities and gone on to find a global cinema audience far wider than that reached by LaBute's soulless and hollow film, if there had not been a core of pure and universal emotion beneath the surface of good-looking people and slick quotable dialogue. Marber has Larry call the human heart 'a fist wrapped in blood' because it lands so many blows on *Closer*'s characters and audience.

Textual Notation

Marber uses a mixture of capitalisation, italics and underlining to indicate how actors should deliver their lines.

Full capitals always indicates increased volume. 'You certainly can't play a capitalised word quietly,' says Marber, as in:

Larry BECAUSE I'M A CAVEMAN.

Underlining indicates emphasis and/or insistence, for example in Scene Four:

Larry She was a <u>woman</u>.

Italics may sometimes indicate emphasis, and always suggests a subtle, fleeting variation from the tone of the rest of a sentence or clause. The altered tone may, to give just three of many examples (all from Scene Four) be accusatory:

Larry Where were *you* between the hours of 5.45 p.m. and 6 p.m., yesterday?

or quizzical:

Larry *Why?* Why would he pretend to be you?

or wry:

Larry I'll say this for him. He can *write*.

Here is how Marber would expect an actress to follow the notation in this line from Scene One:

Alice She must <u>come</u> . . . like a *train* . . . but with <u>*elegance*</u>

'She must emphasise "come" and give a different tone to "train", but I want her to arrive at "elegance" and hit it the hardest. The underline implies a harder tone, an italic is softer than underlining but you still recognise one when you hear it, so "train" must not be hit as hard as "come". "Elegance" is more sensuous, but should be hard as well.'

On the respective lengths of the three-dot ellipses, '*Beat*', '*Pause*' and '*Silence*', he says: 'The shortest is ellipsis. A pause is longer than a beat, which is definitely a shift in thought, and silence is the longest.' When reading the play, these guidelines are particularly useful in imagining the pacing of each scene in performance, and they highlight the vital importance in Marber's writing of the space within, and, especially, between the lines.

In a good stage production this space will be constantly animated, and at times electrified, by the body language and expressions of the actors, which, in conjunction with the dialogue, ensure that the audience senses what the characters are thinking and feeling from moment to moment. For a good illustration of the importance of beats and silence in tracing these gradual shifts within a scene, consider Dan and Anna in Scene Two, from Anna's 'Bad title' to their kiss. The passage allows the gradual build-up of sexual attraction between Anna and Dan to become clearer to the characters and the audience. The intensification is conveyed as much by how the actors fill the gaps between the lines as by the words themselves.

Further Reading and Viewing

Works by Patrick Marber

Dealer's Choice and *After Miss Julie*, in *Plays: 1* (Methuen,
    London, 2004)
Howard Katz (Faber and Faber, London, 2001)
Closer (2004, dir. Mike Nichols; DVD, Sony Pictures Home
    Entertainment)

Reviews and other material on *Closer*

Theatre Record, vol. XVII, 11, pp. 674–9, contains all the
    national newspaper reviews of the Cottesloe production
    of *Closer*
The National Theatre Archive, London, holds a
    comprehensive collection of press reviews, articles,
    programmes and production files on *Closer*, as well as
    recordings of the two NT Platforms on the play and a
    video recording of the Cottesloe production (by
    appointment only) www.nationaltheatre.org.uk/archive

Plays by other writers

Albee, Edward, *Who's Afraid of Virginia Woolf?* (Jonathan
    Cape, London, 1964)
Bovell, Andrew, *Speaking in Tongues* (Currency Press, Sydney,
    1998)
Coward, Noël, *Private Lives* (1930), in *Collected Plays: Two*
    (Methuen, London, 1986)
Mamet, David, *Sexual Perversity in Chicago* (1974), in *Mamet
    Plays: 1* (Methuen, London, 1994)
Pinter, Harold, *Betrayal* (Faber and Faber, London, 1978)
Raine, Craig, *'1953'* (Faber and Faber, London, 1990)

Films on DVD

Carnal Knowledge (1971, dir. Mike Nichols; Momentum
    Pictures)
Lantana [based on Andrew Bovell's *Speaking in Tongues*] (2002,
    dir. Ray Lawrence; Vision Video Ltd)
sex, lies and videotape (1989, dir. Steven Soderbergh; MGM
    Home Entertainment)
Your Friends & Neighbors (1999, dir. Neil LaBute; Universal
    Home Entertainment, Region 1 only)

Closer

For Debra

Closer was first presented in the Cottesloe auditorium of the Royal National Theatre, London, on 22 May 1997. The cast was as follows:

Alice	Liza Walker
Dan	Clive Owen
Larry	Ciaran Hinds
Anna	Sally Dexter

Closer transferred to the Lyttelton auditorium of the Royal National Theatre, London, on 16 October 1997. The cast was as follows:

Alice	Liza Walker
Dan	Mark Strong
Larry	Neil Dudgeon
Anna	Sally Dexter

Closer transferred to the Lyric Theatre in the West End, where it was presented by Robert Fox, on 19 March 1998. The cast was as follows:

Alice	Liza Walker
Dan	Lloyd Owen
Larry	Neil Pearson
Anna	Frances Barber

Director Patrick Marber
Designer Vicki Mortimer
Lighting Hugh Vanstone
Music Paddy Cunneen
Sound Simon Baker
Internet John Owens

Characters

Alice, *a girl from the town.*
Dan, *a man from the suburbs.*
Larry, *a man from the city.*
Anna, *a woman from the country.*

Setting
The play is set in London.

Scene One: January
Scene Two: June (the following year)
Scene Three: January (the following year)
Scene Four: January (the next day)
Scene Five: June (five months later)
Scene Six: June (a year later)
Scene Seven: September (three months later)
Scene Eight: October (a month later)
Scene Nine: November (a month later)
Scene Ten: December (a month later)
Scene Eleven: January (a month later)
Scene Twelve: July (six months later)

The above dates are for information only. They should not be included in any production programme or design.

All settings should be minimal.

Note
This revised version of *Closer* replaces those previously published and is the sole authorised version of the play.

An alternative 'spoken' version of Act One, Scene Three appears at the end of this text.

Act One

Scene One

Hospital.

Early morning. (January.)

Alice *is sitting. She is wearing a black coat. She has a rucksack by her side. Also, an old, brown, leather briefcase.*

She rolls down one sock. She has a cut on her leg, quite bloody. She looks at it. She picks some strands of wool from the wound.

She looks at the briefcase. Thinks. Looks around. Opens it. She searches inside. She pulls out some sandwiches in silver foil. She looks at the contents, smiles, puts them back in the briefcase. Then she removes a green apple from the briefcase. She shines the apple and bites into it.

As she starts to chew **Dan** *enters. He wears a suit and an overcoat. He stops, watches her eating his apple. He is holding two hot drinks in styrofoam cups. After a while she sees him and smiles.*

Alice   Sorry. I was looking for a cigarette.

Dan   I've given up.

He hands her a drink.

Alice   Thanks.

He checks his watch.

Have you got to be somewhere?

Dan   Work.

They sip their drinks.

Didn't fancy my sandwiches?

Alice   I don't eat fish.

Dan   Why not?

Alice   Fish piss in the sea.

Dan   So do children.

Alice   I don't eat children either. What's your work?

Dan   I'm a . . . sort of journalist.

Alice   What *sort*?

Beat.

Dan   I write obituaries.

Beat.

Alice   Do you like it . . . in the *dying* business?

Dan   It's a living.

Alice   Did you grow up in a graveyard?

Dan   Yeah. Suburbia.

Beat.

Alice   Do you think a doctor will come?

Dan   Eventually. Does it hurt?

Alice   I'll live.

Dan   Shall I put your leg up?

Alice   *Why?*

Dan   That's what people do in these situations.

Alice   What is this 'situation'?

They look at each other.

Dan   Do you *want* me to put your leg up?

Alice   Yes, please.

Dan *lifts her leg on to a chair, offers his mobile phone.*

Dan   Is there anyone you'd like to phone?

Alice   I don't know anyone.
Who cut off your crusts?

Dan   Me.

Alice   Did your mother cut off your crusts when you were a little boy?

Dan   I believe she did, yes.

Alice   You should eat your crusts.

Dan   You should stop smoking.

Beat.

Alice   Thank you for scraping me off the road.

Dan   My pleasure.

Alice   You *knight*.

Dan *looks at her.*

Dan   You *damsel.*
Why didn't you look?

Alice   I never look where I'm going.

Dan   We stood at the lights, I looked into your eyes and then you . . . stepped into the road.

Alice   Then what?

Dan   You were lying on the ground, you focused on me, you said, 'Hallo, stranger.'

Alice   What a slut.

Dan   I noticed your leg was cut.

Alice   Did you notice my *legs*?

Dan   Quite possibly.

Alice   Then what?

Dan   The cabbie got out. He crossed himself. He said, 'Thank fuck, I thought I'd killed her.' I said, 'Let's get her to a hospital.' He hesitated . . . (I think he thought there'd be paperwork and he'd be held 'responsible'), so I said, with a slight sneer, 'Please, just drop us at the hospital.'

Alice   Show me the sneer.

Dan *considers then sneers.*

Alice   Very good. *Buster.*

Dan   We put you in the cab and came here.

Alice   What was I doing?

Dan   You were murmuring, 'I'm very sorry for all the inconvenience.' I had my arm round you . . . your head was on my shoulder.

Alice   Was my head . . . *lolling*?

Dan   That's exactly what it was doing.

Pause.

Alice   You'll be late for work.

Dan   Are you saying you want me to go?

Alice   I'm saying you'll be late for work.

Beat.

Dan   Why were you at Blackfriars Bridge?

Alice   I'd been to a club near the meat market . . . *Smithfield.* Do you go clubbing?

Dan   No, I'm too old.

Alice   How old?

Dan   Thirty-five.

Alice   Half-time?

Dan   Thank you very much. So, you were *clubbing* . . .

Alice   Then I went for a walk, I went to see the meat being unloaded.

Dan The carcasses, why?

Alice Because they're repulsive.
Then I found this tiny park . . . it's a graveyard too.
Postman's Park. Do you know it?

Dan No.

Alice There's a memorial to ordinary people who died
saving the lives of others. It's most *curious*.
Then I decided to go to Borough – so I went to Blackfriars
Bridge to cross the river.

Dan That *park* . . . it's near here?

Alice Yes.

Dan Is there a . . . statue?

Alice A Minotaur.

Dan I <u>do</u> know it. We sat there . . . (my mother's dead)
. . . my father and I sat there the afternoon she died.

She died *here*, actually. <u>She</u> was a smoker.

(*Remembering.*) My father . . . ate . . . an egg sandwich . . . his
hands shook with grief . . . pieces of egg fell on the grass . . .
butter on his top lip.

But I don't remember a memorial.

Alice Is your father still alive?

Dan Clinging on. He's in a home.

Alice How did you end up writing obituaries? What did
you *really* want to be?

Dan (*smiles*) Oh . . . I had dreams of being a writer but I
had no voice.
What am I saying? I had no *talent*.
So . . . I ended up in the 'Siberia' of journalism.

Alice Tell me what you do, I want to imagine you in
Siberia.

Dan   Really?

Alice   Yes.

Beat.

Dan   Well . . . we call it 'the obits page'. There's three of us; me, Harry and *Graham*. When I get to work, without fail, Graham will say, 'Who's on the slab?' Meaning, did anyone important die overnight – are you *sure* you want to know?

Alice   <u>Yes</u>.

Dan   Well, if someone 'important' did die we go to the 'deep freeze' which is a computer containing all the obituaries and we'll find the dead person's life.

Alice   People's obituaries are written when they're still alive?

Dan   Some people's.
If no one important has died then *Harry* – he's the editor – he decides who we lead with and we check facts, make calls, polish the prose.
Some days I might be asked to deal with the widows or widowers; they try to persuade us to run an obituary of their husbands or wives. They feel we're dishonouring their loved ones if we don't but . . . most of them are . . . well, there isn't the space.
At six, we stand round the computer and read the next day's page, make final changes, put in a few euphemisms to amuse ourselves . . .

Alice   Such as?

Dan   'He was a convivial fellow', meaning he was an alcoholic.
'He valued his privacy' – gay.
'He *enjoyed* his privacy' . . . raging queen.

Pause. **Alice** *slowly strokes* **Dan***'s face. He is unnerved but not unwilling.*

Alice   And what would your euphemism be?

Dan (*softly*)   For me?

Alice   Mmm.

Dan   He was . . . *reserved.*

Alice   And mine?

Dan   She was . . . *disarming.*

Beat.

Alice   How did you get this job?

Dan   They ask you to write your own obituary: if it amuses, you're in.

They are close. Looking at each other.
Larry *walks past in a white coat.* **Dan** *stops him.*

Dan   Excuse me, we've been waiting quite a long time . . .

Larry   I'm sorry, it's not my . . .

He is about to walk away. He glances briefly at **Alice**. *'Pretty girl.'*
He stops.

What happened?

Alice   I was hit by a cab.

Dan   She was unconscious for about ten seconds.

Larry   May I?

He looks at the wound and examines her leg with interest.

You can feel your toes?

Alice   Yes.

Larry   What's this?

Larry *traces the line of a scar on her leg.*

Alice   It's a scar.

Larry   Yes, I know it's a *scar.* How did you get it?

Alice   In America. A truck.

Larry *looks at the scar.*

Larry   Awful job.

Alice   I was in the middle of nowhere.

Larry   You'll be fine.

Larry *makes to leave.*

Alice   Can I have one?

Larry *looks at her, she nods at his pocket.*

Alice   A cigarette.

Larry *takes out his pack of cigarettes and removes one.*
Alice *reaches for it, he withdraws it.*

Larry   Don't smoke it here.

He hands her the cigarette.

Dan   Thank you.

Larry *exits.* **Alice** *lights the cigarette.*

Alice   Want a drag?

Dan   Yes but no. What were you doing, in 'the middle of nowhere'?

Alice   Travelling.

Beat.

Dan   Alone?

Alice   With . . . a *male*.

Beat.

Dan   What happened to this male?

Alice   I don't know, I ran away.

Dan   Where?

Alice   New York.

Dan   Just like that?

Alice   It's the only way to leave; 'I don't love you any more, goodbye.'

Dan   Supposing you do still love them?

Alice   You don't leave.

Dan   You've never left someone you still love?

Alice   No.

Beat.

Dan   When did you come back?

Alice   Yesterday.

Dan   Where are your belongings?

Alice *points to her rucksack.*

Alice   I'm a waif.

Beat.

Dan   Did you like New York?

Alice   Sure.

Dan   Were you . . . studying?

Alice   *Stripping.*

She looks at him.

Look at your little eyes.

Dan   I can't see my little eyes.

Alice   They're popping out. You're a cartoon.

Beat.

Dan   Were you . . . 'good' at it?

Alice   *Exceptional.*

Dan   Why?

Alice   I know what men want.

Dan   Really?

Alice   Oh yes.

Dan   Tell me . . .

Alice *considers.*

Alice   Men want a girl who looks like a boy.
They want to protect her but she must be a survivor.
And she must <u>come</u> . . . like a *train* . . . but with . . . <u>*elegance*</u>.

What do *you* want?

Pause.

Dan   Who was this . . . *male?*

Alice   A customer. But once I was his he hated me
stripping.

Dan *smiles.*

Dan   What do *you* want?

Alice   To be loved.

Dan   That simple?

Alice   It's a big want.

She looks at him.

Do you have a girlfriend?

Dan   Yeah, *Ruth* . . . she's called Ruth. She's a linguist.

He looks at **Alice**.

Will you meet me after work?

Alice   No, take the day off. Don't go and see '*who's on the
slab*'. I'll call in for you and say you're sick.

Dan   I *can't.*

Alice   Don't be such a pussy.

Dan   I might be anyone, I might be a psychotic.

Alice   I've met psychotics, you're <u>not</u>. *Phone.*

She holds out her hand, **Dan** *gives her his mobile.*

Dan   Memory One.

Alice *punches in the number.*

Alice   Who do I speak to?

Dan   Harry Masters.

Alice   What's your name?

Dan   Mr Daniel Woolf. What's *your* name?

Beat.

Alice   Alice. My name is Alice Ayres.

Blackout.

Scene Two

Anna's *studio.*

Late afternoon. June (the following year).

Anna *stands behind her camera.* **Dan** *sits.* **Anna** *takes a shot.*

Anna   Good.

Shot.

Don't move.

Shots.

Dan   What was this building?

Anna   A refuge for fallen women.

Shot.

Dan   Wasn't there a river here?

Anna   *The Fleet.* They built over it in the eighteenth century.

Dan   A buried river.

Shot.

Anna   If you stand on Blackfriars Bridge you can see where it comes out.

Dan   I think I will.

Anna   You must.

Shot.

Stay there.

Shots.

It inspired an 'urban legend' – a bit like the alligators in New York. People thought that pigs were breeding underground and then one day this big, fat boar swam out into the Thames and trotted off along the Embankment.

Dan   So it was true?

Anna   No, it escaped. From *Smithfield.*

Dan   Pigs can swim?

Anna   Surprisingly well.

Shots.

Relax.

Anna *changes film, adjusts a light, etc.*
Dan *stands up.*

Dan   Do you mind if I smoke?

Anna   If you must.

Dan   I don't have to.

Anna   Then don't.

She looks at **Dan**.

I liked your book.

Dan   Thanks . . .

Anna   When's it published?

Dan   Next year, how come you read it?

Anna   Your publisher sent me a manuscript, I read it last night. You kept me up till *four*.

Dan   I'm flattered.

Anna   Is your anonymous heroine based on someone real?

Beat.

Dan   She's . . . someone called Alice.

Anna   How does she feel about you stealing her life?

Dan   *Borrowing* her life. I'm dedicating the book to her, she's pleased.

He is staring at her, **Anna** *turns, looks at him.*

Pause.

Do you exhibit?

Anna   Next summer.

Dan   Portraits?

Anna   Yes.

Dan   Of who?

Beat.

Anna   Strangers.

Anna *gestures for him to sit again.*
She checks the light on him with a meter.

Dan   How do your strangers feel about *you* stealing *their* lives?

Anna   *Borrowing.*

Anna *adjusts his hair.*

Dan   Am I a stranger?

Anna   No . . . you're a job.

Pause.

Dan   You're beautiful.

Beat.

Anna   No I'm not.

Anna *looks down the lens.*

Chin up, you're a sloucher.

Shots.

Dan   You didn't find it obscene?

Anna   What?

Dan   The book.

Anna   No, I thought it was . . . *accurate.*

Shot.

Dan   About what?

Anna   About sex. About love.

Shot.

Dan   In what way?

Anna   You *wrote* it.

Dan   But you *read* it. Till <u>*four*</u>.

Dan *looks at her,* **Anna** *looks down the lens.*

Anna   Don't raise your eyebrows, you look smug.

Shot.

Stand up.

Dan *stands up.*

Dan   But you did *like* it?

Anna   Yes, but I could go off it.

Shots.

Dan   Any criticisms?

Anna *considers.*

Anna   Bad title.

Dan   Got a better one?

Anna   Really?

Dan   Yeh . . .

Beat.

Anna   'The Aquarium'.

They look at each other.

Beat.

Dan   You liked the dirty bit . . . ?

Anna   Some of it.

Dan   You like aquariums?

Anna   Fish are therapeutic.

Dan   Hang out in aquariums, do you?

Anna   When I can.

Dan   Good for picking up 'Strangers'?

Anna   *Photographing* strangers. I took my first picture in the one at London Zoo.

Silence.

Dan (*gently*)   Come here . . .

Pause.

Anna *moves towards him, slowly. She stops.*

Anna   I don't kiss strange men.

Dan   Neither do I.

They kiss. Ten seconds. **Anna** *slowly pulls back.*

Anna   Do you and this . . . *Alice* . . . live together?

Dan *considers.*

Dan   . . . Yes . . .

Anna (*nods*)   'She has one address in her address book; ours . . . under "H" for home.'

Dan *touches her face.*

Dan   I've cut that line.

Anna   Why?

Dan   Too sentimental.

Anna *gently takes his hand from her face, looks at it and then pulls away from him.*

Dan   Are you married?

Anna   Yes.

Dan *turns away, she looks at him.*

Anna   No.

Dan *turns back.*

Anna   *Yes.*

Dan   <u>Which</u>?

Anna   Separated.

Dan   Do you have any children?

Anna   No.

Dan   Would you like some?

Anna   Yes, but not today.

She shuts her camera case and begins to pack up, session over.

Would *Alice* like children?

Dan   She's too young.

He glances at his watch.

Actually . . . she's coming to meet me here . . . quite soon.

Anna   Why are you wasting her time?

Dan   I'm not. I'm grateful to her . . . she's . . . completely loveable and completely unleaveable.

Anna   And you don't want someone else to get their dirty hands on her?

Beat.

Dan   Maybe.

Anna   Men are crap.

Dan   But all the same . . .

Anna   They're still crap.

The door buzzer goes.

Your muse.

Dan *looks at* **Anna**.

Dan (*ironic*)   You've ruined my life.

Anna   You'll get over it.

They look at each other. **Dan** *goes to exit.*

Dan . . .

Dan *turns.*

Anna   Your shirt.

Dan *exits tucking his shirt into his trousers.*

Silence.

Anna *thinks.*

Dan *enters with* **Alice**. *Her hair is a different colour to Scene One.*

Dan   Anna . . . Alice.

Anna   Hi.

Alice *looks at* **Anna**.

Alice   I'm sorry if you're still working.

Anna   No, we've just finished.

Alice   Was he well-behaved?

Anna   Reasonably.

Alice   Is he photogenic?

Anna   I think so.

Alice   Did you steal his soul?

Anna   Would you like some tea?

Alice   No thanks, I've been serving it all day. Can I use the . . . ?

Anna *(gestures)*   Through there.

Alice *exits.*

Anna   *She* is beautiful.

Dan   Yes, she is.

He looks at **Anna**.

I've got to see you.

Anna   No!

Dan   Why are you getting all . . . 'sisterly'?

Anna   I'm not getting 'sisterly', I don't want trouble.

Dan   I'm not trouble.

Anna   You're taken.

Pause.

Dan   I've *got* to see you.

Anna (*shakes her head*)   <u>Tough</u>.

Pause. **Alice** *enters.*

Alice   I'm a block of ice.

Dan *goes to* **Alice** *and rubs her.*

Alice (*to* **Anna**)   Will you take *my* photo?
I've never been photographed by a professional before.
I'd really appreciate it, I can pay you.

Pause.

Anna   No . . . I'd like to . . .

Alice (*to* **Dan**)   Only if *you* don't mind.

Dan   Why should I?

Alice   Because you'll have to go away.
(*To* **Anna**.) We don't want *him* here while we're working, do
we?

Anna   No, we don't.

Beat.

Dan   . . . *Right* . . . I'll wait in the pub on the corner . . .

He kisses **Alice**.

Have fun.

(*To* **Anna**.) Thank you. Good luck with your exhibition.

Anna   Good luck with your book.

Dan   Thanks.

Dan *exits, lighting a cigarette as he goes.*

Alice   You've got an exhibition?

Anna   Only a small one. Take a seat.

Alice *sits.*
Anna *busies herself with the camera, checks lights, etc.*
Alice *watches her.*

Anna   I read Dan's book, you've had . . . quite a life.

Alice   Thanks.

Are you single?

Anna   . . . Yes.

Alice   Who was your last boyfriend?

Anna *is unsure where this is leading.*

Anna   My husband . . .

Alice   What happened to him?

Beat.

Anna   Someone younger.

Alice   What did he do?

Anna   He made money. In the City.

Alice   We used to get those in the clubs. *Wall Street boys.*

Anna   So . . . these places were quite . . . upmarket?

Alice   Some of them, but I preferred the dives.

Anna   Why?

Alice   The poor are more generous.

Anna *looks into the camera.*

Anna   You've got a great face.

She focuses.

How do you feel about Dan using your life, for his book?

Alice   None of your fucking business.

She stares at **Anna**.

When he let me in . . . downstairs, he had . . . this . . . '*look*'.

I just listened to your . . . *conversation.*

Silence.

Anna   I don't know what to say.

Alice (*gently*)   Take my picture.

Pause.

Anna   I'm not a thief, Alice.

She looks down the lens.

Head up . . .

Alice *raises her head, she is in tears.*

Anna   You look beautiful. Turn to me . . .

She takes her shots. They look at each other.

Good.

Blackout.

Scene Three

Internet.

Early evening. January (the following year).

Dan *is in his flat sitting at a table with a computer. There is a Newton's Cradle on the table. Writerly sloth, etc.*

Larry *is sitting at his hospital desk with a computer. He is wearing a white coat.*

They are in separate rooms.

The scene is silent. Their 'dialogue' appears on a large screen simultaneous to their typing it.

Dan   Hallo.

Larry   hi

Dan   How RU?

Larry   ok

Dan   Cum here often?

Larry   1st time.

Dan   A Virgin. Welcome. What's your name?

Larry   Larry. U?

Dan *considers.*

Dan   Anna

Larry   Nice 2 meet U

Dan   I love COCK

Pause.

Larry   Youre v.forward

Dan   And UR chatting on 'LONDON FUCK'. Do U want sex?

Larry   yes. describe u.

Dan   Dark hair. Dirty mouth. Epic Tits.

Larry   define epic

Dan   36DD

Larry   Nice arse?

Dan   Y

Larry   Becos i want 2 know

Dan *smiles.*

Dan   No, 'Y' means 'Yes'.

Larry   O

Dan   I want 2 suck U senseless.

Larry   B my guest

Dan   Sit on my face Fuckboy.

Larry   I'm there

Dan   Wear my wet knickers.

Beat.

Larry   ok

Dan   RU well hung?

Larry   9£

Larry (*speaking*)   Shit.

Larry (*typing*)   9″

Dan   GET IT OUT

Larry *considers and then unzips. He puts his hand in his trousers. The phone on his desk rings. Loud. He jumps.*

Larry (*speaking*)   Wait.

Larry (*typing*)   wait

Larry *picks up the phone.* **Dan** *lights a cigarette.*

Larry (*speaking*)   <u>Yes</u>. What's the histology? *Progressive?* Sounds like an atrophy.

Larry *puts the phone down and goes back to his keyboard.* **Dan** *clicks the balls on his Newton's Cradle.*

Larry   hallo?

Dan *looks at his screen.*

Larry   anna

Larry (*speaking*)   Bollocks.

Larry (*typing*)   ANNA? WHERE RU?

Dan   Hey, big Larry, what d'you wank about?

Larry *considers.*

Larry   Ex-girlfriends.

Dan   Not current g-friends?

Larry   Never

Dan *smiles.*

Dan   Tell me your sex-ex fantasy . . .

Larry   Hotel room . . . they tie me up . . . tease me . . . won't let me come. They fight over me, 6 tonges on my cock, ballls, perineum etc.

Dan   All hail the Sultan of Twat?

Larry *laughs.*

Larry   Anna, wot do U wank about?

Dan *thinks.*

Dan   Strangers.

Larry   details . . .

Dan   They form a Q and I attend to them like a cum hungry bitch,1 in each hole and both hands.

Larry   then?

Dan   They cum in my mouth arse tits cunt hair.

Larry *(speaking)*   Jesus.

Larry*'s phone rings. He picks up the receiver and replaces it without answering. Then he takes it off the hook.*

Larry *(typing)*   then?

Dan   i lik it off like the dirty slut I am. Wait,have to type with 1 hand . . . I'm cumming right now . . . ohohohohohohohohohohohohohohohohohohohoooooooo ooooooooooooooooooooooooooooooooooooooooooooooooo +_)(*&^%$£"!_*)&%^&!"!"£$%%^^%&^%&&*&*((*(*)&^ %*((£££

Pause. **Larry***, motionless, stares at his screen.*

Larry   was it good?

Dan   No.

Larry *shakes his head.*

Larry   I'm shocked

Dan   PARADISE SHOULD BE SHOCKING

Larry   RU4 real?

Beat.

Dan   MEET ME

Pause.

Larry   serious?

Dan   Y

Larry   when

Dan   NOW

Larry   can't. I'm a Dr. Must do rounds.

Dan *smiles.* **Larry** *flicks through his desk diary.*

Dan   Don't b a pussy. Life without riskisdeath. Desire,like the world,is am accident. The bestsex is anon. We liv as we dream,ALONE. I'll make u cum like a train.

Larry   Tomorrow,1 pm,where?

Dan *thinks.*

Dan   The Aquarium, London Zoo & then HOTEL.

Larry   How will U know me?

Dan   Bring white coat

Larry   ?

Dan   Dr + Coat = Horn 4 me

Larry   !

Dan   I send U a rose my love . . .

Larry   ?

Dan   (@)

Larry   Thanks. CU at Aquarium. Bye Anna.

Dan   Bye Larry xxxxx

Larry   xxxxxx

They look at their screens.

Blackout.

Scene Four

Aquarium.

Afternoon. January (the next day).

Anna *is sitting on a bench, alone. She has a camera. She looks at the fish, occasionally referring to her guide book.*

Larry *enters.*
He sees **Anna**. *He checks her out and smiles.*
Anna *sees him and vaguely nods, acknowledging his presence.*

Larry   Anna?

Anna   . . . Yes . . . ?

Larry *unbuttons his overcoat and holds it open. He is wearing his white coat underneath.*

Larry   I've got 'The Coat'.

Anna *observes him.*

Anna   Yes, you *have*.

Larry   'The White Coat.'

Anna   So I see . . .

Larry   I'm Larry. (*Dirty.*) 'The Doctor.'

Beat.

Anna   Hallo, Doctor Larry.

Larry   Feel free to call me . . . '*The Sultan*'.

Anna   *Why?*

Larry (*laughs*)   I can't believe these things actually *happen*. I thought . . . if you turned up, you'd be a bit of a trout . . . but you're bloody gorgeous.

Anna   Thanks.

Beat.

Larry   You mentioned a hotel . . .

Anna *looks at him, trying to work out who he is.*

Larry   No rush.

He checks his watch.

Actually, there *is*, I've got to be in surgery by three.

Anna   Are you having an operation?

Larry (*laughs*)   No, I'm *doing* one.

Anna   You really *are* a doctor?

Larry   I said I was. (*Sudden panic.*) You are . . . _Anna_?

Anna   Yes. I'm sorry, have we met somewhere?

Larry   Don't play games, you . . . 'Nymph of the Net'. (*Confused.*) You were filthy *yesterday*.

Anna   Was I?

Larry   YES. 'Wear my wet knickers', 'Sit on my face', 'I'm a cum hungry bitch typing with one . . .'

Anna *smiles.*

Larry   Why do I feel like a pervert?

Anna   I think . . . you're the victim . . . of a medic's prank.

Pause.

Larry   I am *so* sorry.

Larry *exits.* **Anna** *chuckles.* **Larry** *re-enters.*

Larry   NO. We spoke on the Net but now you've *seen* me you don't . . . it's *fine*, I'm not going to get <u>upset</u> about it.

Anna   Then why are you upset?

Larry   I'm not, I'm <u>frustrated</u>.

Anna   I don't even have a computer, I'm a photographer.

Larry *considers.*

Larry   Where were *you* between the hours of 5.45 and 6.00 p.m., yesterday?

Anna   I was in a café seeing . . . an acquaintance.

Larry   Name?

Anna   Alice Ayres.

Larry   The nature of your business?

Anna (*amused*)   Photographic business. Where were *you* between those hours?

Larry   On the Net talking to you.

Anna   No.

Larry   Well, I was talking to *someone*.

Anna (*realising*)   Pretending to *be* me.

You were talking to Daniel Woolf.

Larry   Who?

Anna   He's Alice's boyfriend. She told me yesterday that he plays around on the Net. It's _him_.

Larry   No, I was talking to a woman.

Anna   How do you know?

Larry   Because . . . believe me, she was a woman, I got a _huge_ . . . She was a <u>woman</u>.

Anna   No, she wasn't.

Larry   She wasn't, was she.

Anna   No.

Larry   What a CUNT. Sorry.

Anna   I'm a grown-up, 'Cunt Away'.

Larry   Thanks. This . . . '_bloke_' . . .

Anna   Daniel Woolf.

Larry   How do you know him?

Anna   I don't know him really, I took his photo for a book he wrote.

Larry   I hope it sank without trace.

Anna   It's on its way.

Larry   There is justice in the world. What's it called?

Anna (_smiles_)   'The Aquarium'.

Larry   What a PRICK. He's <u>advertising</u>!
Why? Why would he pretend to be you?

Anna   He likes me.

Larry   Funny way of showing it, can't he send you flowers?

He produces a crumpled rose from his coat pocket. He hands it to
Anna.

Here.

Anna   . . . Thanks . . .

She looks at the rose, then at **Larry**.

Wonderful thing, the Internet.

Larry   Oh yes.

Anna   The possibility of genuine global communication, the first great democratic medium.

Larry   Absolutely, it's the future.

Anna   Two boys tossing in cyberspace.

Larry   *He* was the tosser.

I'll say this for him, he can *write*.

He looks at **Anna**.

Is he in love with you?

Anna   I don't know. No.

Larry   Are you in love with him?

Anna   I hardly know him, no.

Larry   But you're sort of . . . interested?

Anna   I think he's . . . *interesting*.

Beat.

Larry   So what are you doing here?

Pause.

Anna   Looking at fish.

Anna *looks away from him.*

Larry (*gently*)   Are you all right?

Anna *nods.*

Larry   You can tell me . . .

Anna   Because you're a doctor?

Larry   Because I'm *here*.

Anna *turns to him.*

Larry   Crying is allowed.

Anna   I'm not allowed. Thanks, anyway.

Larry   I'm famed for my bedside manner.

Anna *raises her camera,* **Larry** *covers his face.*

Larry   Don't, I look like a criminal in photos.

Anna   Please, it's my birthday.

Larry (*dropping his hands*)   Really?

Anna *takes his photo.*

Anna   Yes. (*Rueful.*) Really.

They look at each other.

Larry   Happy birthday.

Blackout.

Scene Five

Gallery.

Evening. June (five months later).

Alice *is looking at a huge photograph of herself. She has a bottle of lager. She wears a black dress.*

Dan *has a glass of wine. A slightly shabby black suit. He looks at* **Alice** *looking at the image.*

Dan   Cheers.

She turns. They drink. **Dan** *admires the photo.*

You're the belle of the bullshit. You look beautiful.

Alice   I'm *here.*

Dan *looks at* **Alice,** *smiles.*

Alice   A man came into the café today and said, 'Hey, *waitress,* what are you waiting for?'

Dan   Funny guy.

Alice   I said, 'I'm waiting for a man to come in here and *fuck me sideways* with a beautiful line like that.'

Dan (*smiles*)   What did he do?

Alice   He asked for a cup of tea with two sugars.

She looks at him.

I'm waiting for *you.*

Dan   To do what?

Beat.

Alice (*gently*)   Leave me.

Dan (*concerned*)   I'm not going to leave you. I totally love you. What is this?

Alice   Please let me come . . .

Dan *turns away.*

Alice   I want to *be there* for you. Are you ashamed of me?

Dan   Of course not. I've told you, I want to be alone.

Alice   Why?

Dan   To *grieve* . . . to think.

Alice   I love you, why won't you let me?

Dan   It's only a weekend.

Alice   Why won't you let me *love* you?

Silence.

We've never spent a weekend in the country.

Dan   Well . . . we will.

He turns, drinks. He looks offstage and smiles at something he sees.

Harry's here . . . pissed as a newt.

He wants me to go back to 'obits' . . . says they miss me.

Alice   Poor Harry, you know he's in love with you.

Dan   No he's not.

He glances offstage again.

Is he?

Alice (*smiles*)   <u>Yes</u>. Do you want to go back?

Dan   We're very poor . . .

Alice   What about your writing?

Dan *shrugs.*

Dan   Look . . . I'm going to say hallo and goodbye to Anna and then I'll get a cab to the station, OK?

Buster?

I love you.

He kisses her forehead.

Alice (*softly*)   Kiss my lips . . .

Dan   Sorry.

He kisses her on the lips.

I'll call you as soon as I get there.

Dan *exits as* **Larry** *enters. They almost collide.*
Larry *regards the departing* **Dan**.

Alice *lights a cigarette, she uses her bottle as an ashtray.*

Larry *is wearing a suit with a black cashmere sweater with a collar. He has a bottle of wine and a glass.*
Alice *looks at him, curious.*

Larry   Evening.

Alice   Are you a waiter?

Larry   No, I'm a refugee escaping from the glittering babble.

He looks at the photo and then at his exhibition price list.

And . . . *you* are . . . *'Young Woman, London'*.

He looks at **Alice**.

Pricey. Do you like it?

Alice   No.

Larry   Well, you should. What were you so sad about?

Alice   Life.

Larry   What's that then?

Alice *smiles*.

Larry (*gesturing to the photos*)   What d'you reckon, in general?

Alice   You want to talk about *art*?

Larry   I know it's *vulgar* to discuss 'The Work' at an opening of 'The Work' but *someone's* got to do it. Serious, what d'you think?

Alice   It's a lie.
It's a bunch of sad strangers photographed beautifully and all the rich <u>fuckers</u> who appreciate *art* say it's beautiful because that's what they <u>want</u> to see.
But the people in the photos are sad and alone but the pictures make the world *seem* beautiful.
So, the exhibition is <u>reassuring</u>, which makes it a lie, and everyone loves a <u>Big Fat Lie</u>.

Larry   I'm the Big Fat Liar's boyfriend.

Alice   Bastard!

Larry   Larry.

Alice   Alice.

Beat. **Alice** *moves in on him.*

So . . . you're Anna's boyfriend?

Larry   A princess can kiss a frog.

Alice   How long have you been seeing her?

Larry   Four months. We're in 'the first flush'.
It's <u>Paradise</u>. All my nasty habits amuse her . . .

He gazes at **Alice**.

You shouldn't smoke.

Alice   Fuck off.

Larry   I'm a doctor, I'm supposed to say things like that.

Alice *now realises where she's seen him before. She holds out her packet of cigarettes.*

Alice   Want one?

Larry   <u>No</u>.

Alice *continues to offer the packet.*

Larry   *Yes.* No. Fuck it, <u>yes</u>. NO. I've given up.

He watches her smoking.

Pleasure and self-destruction, the perfect poison.

Alice *gives him a dirty smile.*

Larry   Anna told me your bloke wrote a book, any good?

Alice   Of course.

Larry   It's about *you*, isn't it?

Alice   Some of me.

Larry   Oh? What did he leave out?

Beat.

Alice   The truth.

Beat.

Larry   Is he here? Your *bloke.*

Alice   Yeah, he's talking to your *bird.*

Larry *glances offstage, thinks, then returns to* **Alice**.

Larry   *So* . . . you were a stripper?

Alice (*flirtatious*)   Yeah . . . *and* ?

Larry *sees the scar on her leg.*

Larry   Mind if I ask how you got that?

Beat.

Alice   You've asked me this before.

Larry   When?

Alice   Two and a half years ago. I was in hospital. You
looked at my leg.

Larry   How did you remember me?

Alice   It was a memorable day.
You didn't really want to stop but you did, you were off for
a crafty smoke.
You gave me a cigarette.

Larry   Well, I don't smoke now and nor should you.

Alice   But you *used* to go and smoke. *On the sly.*

Larry   Yeah, in a little park near the hospital.

Alice   *Postman's Park?*

Larry   That's the one.

Alice *takes a swig from his bottle.*

Larry   And . . . the *scar?*

Alice   A mafia hit man broke my leg.

Larry (*disbelieving*)   Really?

Alice   Absolutely.

Larry   Doesn't look like a break . . .

Alice   What does it look like?

Larry   Like something went into it. (*Tentative.*) A knife, maybe . . .

Alice   When I was eight . . . some metal went into my leg when my parents' car crashed . . . when they *died*. Happy now?

Larry   Sorry, it was none of my business. I'm supposed to be off duty.

Alice *looks at him.*

Alice   Is it nice being good?

Larry   I'm not good.

He looks at her, close.

What about *you*?

He gently strokes her face, she lets him.

I'm seeing my first private patient tomorrow. Tell me I'm not a sell-out.

Alice   You're not a sell-out.

Larry   *Thanks.* You take care.

Alice   I will, you too.

Alice *exits.* **Larry** *watches her go.*
Larry *exits as* **Dan** *enters elsewhere.*
Dan *carries a small suitcase. He checks his watch and waits, nervously.*

Anna *enters.*

Pause. They look at each other.

Anna   I can't talk for long.

Dan   Bit of a do, isn't it?

Anna   Yeah, I hate it.

Dan   But you're *good* at it.

So, he's a *dermatologist.* Can you get more boring than that?

Anna   Obituarist?

Dan   Failed novelist, please.

Anna   I was sorry about your book.

Dan   Thanks, I blame the title.

Anna (*smiles*)   I blame the critics. You must write another one.

Dan   Why can't failure be attractive?

Anna   It's not a failure.

Dan   It's *perceived* to be, therefore it is. Pathetically, I needed praise. A *real* writer is . . . above such concerns.

Anna   Romantic tosh.

Dan   Ever had bad reviews? Well, shut up then.

Talk to *Doctor Larry* about photography, do you?

Is he a fan of Man Ray or Karsh?

He'll <u>bore</u> you.

Anna   No he won't – he <u>doesn't</u>, actually.

Dan (*exasperated*)   I cannot believe I made this happen.

What were you <u>doing</u> at the Aquarium?

(*Joking.*) Thinking of me?

Anna   No. How's Alice?

Dan   She's fine. Do you love him?

Anna   Yes, very much.

Beat.

Dan (*alarmed*)   You're not going to *marry* him?

Anna   I might.

Dan   *Don't.* Marry me. Children, everything.
You don't want <u>his</u> children – three little stooges in white coats.
Don't marry him, marry me.
Grow old with me . . . *die* with me . . . wear a battered cardigan on the beach in Bournemouth.
Marry me.

Anna (*smiles*)   I don't *know* you.

Dan   <u>Yes you do</u>.
I couldn't feel what I feel for you unless you felt it too.
Anna, *we're in love* – it's not our fault, stop wasting his time.

Anna   I haven't *seen* you for a <u>year</u>.

Dan   <u>Yes you have</u>.

Anna   Only because you *stalked* me outside my studio.

Dan   I didn't <u>stalk</u> . . . I . . . *lurked*.
And when I wasn't there you looked for me.

Anna   How do you know, if you weren't *there*?

Dan   Because I <u>was</u> there . . . lurking from a distance.
(I love your work, by the way, it's tragic).

Anna (*sarcastic*)   Thanks.

Dan *gestures to his suitcase.*

Dan   I know this isn't 'appropriate', I'm going to my father's funeral – <u>come with me</u>.

Anna   Your father died?

Dan   It's fine, I hated him – no, I didn't – I don't <u>care</u>, I *care* about <u>THIS</u>.
Come with me, spend a weekend with me, then decide.

Anna   I don't want to go to your father's funeral.
There's nothing to . . . *<u>decide</u>*.
What about Alice?

Dan   She'll <u>survive</u>.

I can't be her father any more.

Anna, you want to believe he's . . . 'the one' . . . it's not *real*, you're scared of *<u>this</u>*.

Anna   There is no '<u>this</u>'. I <u>love</u> him.

Dan   *Why?*

Anna   Any number of reasons!

Dan   Name *one*.

Anna   He's kind.

Dan (*ferocious*)   Don't give me 'kind'. 'Kind' is *dull*, 'kind' will kill you. Alice is '*kind*', even *I'm* '<u>kind</u>', anyone can be fucking KIND.

(*Gently.*) I cannot live without you.

Anna   You can . . . you *do*.

Beat.

Dan   This is not me, I don't do this.

All the language is old, there are no new words . . . *I love you.*

Beat.

Anna   No, you don't.

Dan   Yes . . . I do. I *need* you.
I can't think, I can't work, I can't *breathe*.
We are going to *<u>die</u>*.
Please . . . *save* me.

Look at me.

Anna *looks at* **Dan**.

Dan   Tell me you're not in love with me.

Beat.

Anna   I'm not in love with you.

Pause.

Dan   You just lied.
See me next week. *Please*, Anna . . . I'm begging you . . . *I'm*
your stranger . . . <u>*jump*</u>.

Silence. They are very close. **Larry** *has entered, he is looking at them.*
Dan *sees him and goes to exit.*

Anna   Your case.

Dan *returns, picks up his suitcase and exits.*

Pause.

Larry   Hallo . . . *Stranger.*

Anna   Hallo.

Larry   Intense conversation?

Beat.

Anna   His father's died. Were you *spying*?

Larry   Lovingly *observing* – (with a telescope).

He kisses **Anna**.

He's taller than his photo.

Anna   The photo's a head shot.

Larry   Yeah, I know, but his head *implied* a short body . . .
but in fact, his head is . . . deceptive.

Anna   Deceptive?

Larry   Yes, because he's actually got a *long* body. He's a stringy fucker.

Anna *laughs.*

Larry   I could 'ave 'im.

Anna   *What?*

Larry   If it came to it, in a scrap, I could 'ave 'im.

Anna *smiles.*

Larry   Did you tell him we call him 'Cupid'?

Anna   No, that's *our* joke.

Anna *tugs his sweater, pulling him towards her.*

Larry   I've never worn cashmere before. Thank you. I'm Cinderella at the ball.

Anna (*charmed*)   You're such a peasant.

Larry   You love it.

He holds her.

I had a chat with young Alice.

Anna   Fancy her?

Larry   Course. Not as much as *you.*

Anna   Why?

Larry   You're a woman . . . she's a girl.
She has the moronic beauty of youth but she's got . . . *side.*

Anna   She seems very open to me.

Larry   That's how she *wants* to seem.
You forget you're dealing with a clinical observer of the human carnival.

Anna   Am I now?

Larry   Oh yes.

Anna   You seem more like 'the cat who got the cream'.
You can stop licking yourself, you know.

Pause. **Anna** *turns to* **Larry**, *slowly.*

Larry (*coolly*)   That's the nastiest thing you've ever said to
me.

Anna   God, I'm sorry. It was a <u>horrible</u> thing to say. It's
just . . . my family's here and friends . . .
I have no excuse. I'm sorry.

Pause.

Larry   Forget it. I know what you mean. I'll stop pawing
you.

Anna *kisses him.*

Larry   I met your *Dad* . . .

Anna   I know. He actually said, 'I like him.' He's never
said that before . . . about *anyone.* They all adored you; my
stepmother thinks you're gorgeous, 'Lovely hands,' she said,
'you can imagine him doing his stitching, very sensitively.'

Larry   So they didn't think I was 'beneath you'?

Anna   *No.* You're not . . . you're *you* and you're wonderful.

Larry *holds her.*

Larry   Did you like my folks? They loved *you.*

Anna   Your mother's got such a . . . kind face.

They look at each other.

Blackout.

Scene Six

Domestic interiors.

Midnight. June (a year later).

Anna *sitting on a chaise longue.*

Alice *asleep, curled up on a small sofa. She is wearing striped pyjamas. A half-eaten red apple beside her.*

They are in separate rooms.

Dan *enters. He carries the brown briefcase seen in Scene One.*
He looks at **Alice**.
After a while she wakes.

Alice   Where've you been?

What?

Dan   Work. I had a drink with Harry. You never have *one* drink with Harry.

Alice   Did you eat? I made sandwiches – no crusts.

Dan   I'm not hungry.

Pause.

Alice   *What?*

Beat.

Dan   This will hurt.

I've been with Anna.

I'm in love with her. We've been seeing each other for a year.

Silence.

Alice *gets up and slowly exits.*

On the other side of the stage **Larry** *enters.*
He has a suitcase, bags, duty-free carrier.

Larry (*to* **Anna**)   Don't move!
I want to remember this moment for ever: the first time I walked through the door, returning from a business trip, to be greeted by my *wife*.
I have, in this moment, become an adult.

He kisses **Anna**.

Thanks for waiting up, you darling. You goddess.
I missed you.
Jesus, I'm knackered.

Anna   Didn't you sleep on the plane?

Larry   No, because the permed German sleeping next to
me was snoring like a *Messerschmitt*.

He removes his jacket, **Anna** *takes it.*

What's the time?

Anna   Midnight.

Larry   Seven.
Time: what a tricky little fucker.
My head's in two places, my brain actually *hurts*.

Anna   Do you want some food?

Larry   Nahh, I ate my 'Scooby Snacks' on the plane. I
need a bath.

Anna   Shall I run you one?

Larry   No, I'll just have a shower.

He untucks his shirt and kicks off his shoes.

You OK?

Anna   Mmhmm.

Beat. They look at each other.

How was the . . . *thing*?

Larry   As dermatological conferences go, it was a riot.

Larry *takes a bottle of Scotch from his bag of duty-free and swigs it.*

Anna   How was the hotel?

Larry   Someone told me that the beautiful people of '*The Paramount Hotel*', the concierge and the bell boys and girls – did you know this? They're all *whores*.

Anna   Everyone knows that.

Larry   *I* didn't. Want some?

He offers the bottle, **Anna** *takes a swig.*

I *love* New York. What a town: it's a twenty-four-hour pageant called, 'Whatever You Want.'
Then, you arrive back at Heathrow and the first thing you see is this . . . *carpet.*
This Unbelievable <u>Carpet</u>.
What the fuck colour is the carpet at Heathrow Airport?
They must've laid it to reassure foreigners we're not a serious country.

God, I stink.

Anna   Are you all right?

Larry   Yeah. I don't suppose you fancy a friendly poke?

Beat.

Anna   I've just had a bath.

Larry   I'll see to myself then, in the *Elle Decoration* bathroom.

Anna   You chose that bathroom.

Larry   Yeah and every time I wash in it I feel *dirty*. It's *cleaner* than I am. It's got <u>attitude</u>. The mirror says, 'Who the fuck are you?'

Anna   You chose it.

Larry   Doesn't mean I like it. We shouldn't have . . . *this.*

Larry *gestures vaguely about the room.*

Anna   Are you experiencing bourgeois guilt?

Beat.

Larry (*sharp*)   Working-class guilt.

He looks at **Anna**.

Why are you dressed? If you've just had a bath.

Beat.

Anna   We needed some milk.

Larry   Right.

He goes to exit, stops.

You OK?

Anna   Uhhuh. You?

Larry   Yeah . . .

Larry *exits.*
Alice *enters. She is wearing the black coat from Scene One, also her rucksack from the same scene.*

Alice   I'm going.

Dan   I'm sorry.

Alice   Irrelevant. What are you sorry for?

Beat.

Dan   Everything.

Alice   Why didn't you tell me before?

Beat.

Dan   Cowardice.

Alice   Is it because she's clever?

Dan   No, it's because . . . she doesn't need me.

Pause.

Alice   Do you bring her here?

Dan   Yes.

Alice   She sits here?

Dan   Yes.

Beat.

Alice   Didn't she get *married*?

Dan   She stopped seeing me.

Beat.

Alice   Is that when we went to the country? To celebrate our third anniversary?

Dan   Yes.

Alice   <u>At least have the guts to look at me</u>.

Dan *looks at her.*

Alice   Did you phone her? To beg her to come back? When you went for your 'long, *lonely* walks'?

Dan   Yes.

Alice   You're a piece of shit.

Dan   Deception is brutal, I'm not pretending otherwise.

Alice   How . . . ? How does it *work*? How can you do this to someone?

Silence.

Dan   I don't know.

Alice   Not good enough, I'm going.

Dan *prevents her from leaving.*

Dan   It's late, it's not *safe* out there.

Alice   And it's *safe* in here?

Dan   What about your things?

Alice   I don't need 'things'.

Dan   Where will you go?

Alice   I'll disappear.

Larry *enters having had his shower. He is wearing a dressing-gown. He hands* **Anna** *a shoebox.*

Larry   'The Sultan' has returned bearing gifts.

Anna *opens the box and takes out the shoes.*

Dan *moves towards* **Alice**.

Alice   DON'T COME NEAR ME.

Anna (*to* **Larry**)   They're beautiful. Thank you.

Larry *kisses* **Anna**.

Larry   Hey, guess what, *Alice* was at the Paramount Hotel.

Anna   What?

Larry   They sell arty postcards in the lobby, I bought one to boost your sales.

Larry *takes a postcard from his dressing-gown pocket and reads the back.*

'Young Woman, London'.

He hands the postcard to **Anna**.

And . . . I checked for your book in 'The Museum of Modern Art'. It's <u>there</u>. Someone bloody bought one! This *student* with a ridiculous little beard, he was drooling over your photo on the inside cover – fancied you, the *Geek*. I was so proud of you – 'You've Broken New York.'

Anna   You're wonderful.

Larry   Don't ever forget it.

Larry *exits.*

Alice   Change your mind.

Please, change your mind.

Can I still see you?

Dan . . . can I still see you?

Answer me.

Dan   I can't see you. If I see you I'll never leave you.

Beat.

Alice   What will you do if *I* find someone else?

Dan   Be jealous.

Beat.

Alice   Do you still fancy me?

Dan   Of course.

Alice *shakes her head.*

Alice   You're lying. I've been '*you*'.

She starts to cry.

Hold me?

Dan *holds her.*

Alice   I amuse you but I bore you.

Dan   No. *No*.

Alice   You did love me?

Dan   I'll *always* love you. You changed my life. I hate hurting you.

Alice   So why are you?

Dan   Because . . . I'm selfish and I think I'll be happier with her.

Alice   You won't, you'll miss me. No one will ever love you as much as I do.

Dan   I know.

Pause.

Alice   Why isn't love enough?

I'm the one who leaves.

I'm supposed to leave *you*.

I'm the one who leaves.

She kisses **Dan**. *He responds. She breaks.*

Make some tea . . . *Buster.*

Dan *exits.*
Alice *and* **Anna** *are alone.*
Larry *enters. He is wearing trousers and the black cashmere seen in Scene Five.*

Anna   Why are you dressed?

Larry   Because I think you might be about to leave me and I didn't want to be wearing a dressing-gown.

I slept with someone in New York.
A whore.
I'm sorry.

Please don't leave me.

Beat.

Anna   Why?

Larry   For sex. I wanted *sex.* (I wore a condom.)

Beat.

Anna   Was it . . . good?

Larry *huffs and puffs.*

Larry   . . . Yes . . .

Anna   '*Paramount*' whore?

Larry   No . . . Forty . . . something Street.

Anna   Where did you go?

Larry   Her place.

Anna   Nice?

Larry   Not as nice as ours. I'm really sorry.

Pause.

Anna   Why did you tell me?

Larry   I couldn't lie to you.

Anna   Why not?

Larry   Because I love you.

Pause.

Anna   It's fine.

Larry   Really? *Why?*

Anna *looks at her shoes.*

Anna   Guilt present?

Larry   Love present. Something's wrong . . .
Anna . . .

Anna *turns to him.*

Larry   Are you leaving me?

Anna *nods.*

Larry   Why?

Anna   Dan.

Beat.

Larry   'Cupid'? He's our *joke.*

Anna   I love him.

Pause.

Larry   You're seeing him now . . .

Anna   Yes.

Larry   Since when?

Anna   Since my opening, last year. I'm disgusting.

Beat.

Larry   You're *phenomenal* . . . you're so . . . <u>clever</u>.

Why did you marry me?

Anna   I stopped seeing him, I wanted us to work.

Larry   Why did you tell me you wanted children?

Anna   Because I did.

Larry   And now you want children with him?

Anna   Yes – I don't know – I'm so sorry.

Pause.

Larry   <u>*Why?*</u>

Beat.

Anna   I need him.

Silence.

Larry   But . . . we're happy . . . aren't we?

Anna   Yes.

Beat.

Larry   Are you going to live with him?

Anna   Yes. You stay here, if you want to.

Larry   I don't give a FUCK about 'the spoils'.

Alice *exits with her rucksack.*

Larry   You did this the day we <u>met</u>; let me *hang* myself for your amusement. Why didn't you tell me the second I walked in the door.

Anna   I was scared.

Larry   Because you're a <u>coward</u>. You spoilt *bitch*.

Dan *enters with two cups of tea, he sees* **Alice** *has gone. He exits after her.*

Larry   Are you dressed because you thought I might hit you?

He moves towards **Anna**, *slowly.*

(*Close.*) What do you think I *am*?

Anna   I've been hit before.

Larry   Not by me.

He stands over **Anna**.

Is he a good fuck?

Anna   Don't do this.

Larry   Just answer the question. Is he *good*?

Beat.

Anna   Yes.

Larry   Better than me?

Anna   Different.

Larry   <u>Better</u>?

Anna   Gentler.

Larry   What does that mean?

Anna   You know what it means.

Larry   *Tell me.*

Anna   No.

Larry   I treat you like a whore?

Anna   Sometimes.

Larry   Why would that be?

Silence.

Anna   I'm sorry, you're –

Larry   <u>Don't say it</u>, don't fucking say, 'You're too good for me.' I *am* – <u>but don't say it</u>.

He kneels to her.

(*Gently.*) Anna, you're making the mistake of your life. You're leaving me because you think you don't deserve happiness, but you do, Anna, you do . . .

He looks at her.

Did you have a bath because you had sex with him?

Anna *looks at him. He moves away from her.*

Larry   So you didn't smell of him? So you'd feel less *guilty*?

And how do you *feel*?

Anna   Guilty.

Beat.

Larry   Did you ever love me?

Anna   *Yes*.

Larry   Big fucking deal.

Silence. **Larry** *breaks down.*

Anna . . . please, don't leave me . . . *please*.

Anna *holds* **Larry**.

On the other side of the stage **Dan** *re-enters and sits on the sofa.*

Larry   Did you do it here?

Anna   No.

Larry   Why not?

He breaks from her.

(*Hard.*) Just tell me the truth.

Beat.

Anna   Yes, we did it here.

Larry   Where?

Beat.

Anna   Here.

Larry   On this?

He gestures to the chaise longue.

We had our first fuck on this.

Think of *me*?

When?

When did you do it here?

ANSWER THE QUESTION.

Beat.

Anna (*scared*)   This evening.

Pause.

Larry   Did you come?

Anna   Why are you doing this?

Larry   Because I want to know.

Beat.

Anna (*softly*)   Yes . . . I came.

Larry   How many times?

Anna   Twice.

Larry   How?

Anna   First he went down on me and then we fucked.

Beat.

Larry   Who was where?

Anna (*tough*)   I was on top and then he fucked me from behind.

Larry   And that's when you came the second time?

Anna   *Why is the sex so important?*

Larry   BECAUSE I'M A FUCKING CAVEMAN.

Did you touch yourself while he fucked you?

Anna   Yes.

Larry   You wank for him?

Anna   Sometimes.

Larry   And he does?

Anna   We do everything that people who have sex do.

Larry   You enjoy sucking him off?

Anna   *Yes.*

Larry   You like his cock?

Anna   I love it.

Larry   You like him coming in your face?

Anna   *Yes.*

Larry   What does it taste like?

Anna   It tastes like you but *sweeter*.

Larry   THAT's the *spirit*. Thank you. Thank you for your *honesty*.
Now fuck off and die. You fucked-up slag.

Blackout.

Act Two

Scene Seven

Lapdance club.

Late night. September (three months later).

Larry *is sitting. He is wearing a smart suit.*

Alice *is standing. She is wearing a short dress, wig and high heels. She has a garter round her thigh, there is cash in the garter.*

They are in a private room. Music in the distance.

Larry *gazes at her. She smiles. She is nice to him.*

Silence.

Larry   I love you.

Pause.

Alice   Thank you.

Beat.

Larry   What's this room called?

Alice   'The Paradise Suite'.

Larry   How many Paradise Suites are there?

Alice   Six.

Beat.

Larry   Do I have to pay you to talk to me?

Alice   No, but if you want to tip me it's your choice.

He takes out a twenty. She presents her leg. He puts the money in her garter.

Thank you.

Larry   I went to a place like this in New York.

This is *swish*.
Pornography has gone upmarket – BULLY FOR
ENGLAND.
This is honest *progress*, don't you think?

Alice   England always imports the best of America.

Larry   I used to come here twenty years ago . . . it was a
punk club . . . the stage was . . .

He can't remember, he gives up.

Everything is a Version of Something Else.

He takes a slug of his drink.

Twenty years ago, how old were *you*?

Alice   Four.

Larry   Christ, when I was in flares you were in nappies.

Alice   My nappies were flared.

Larry *laughs.*

Larry   You have the face of an angel.

Alice   Thank you.

Larry   What does your cunt taste like?

Alice   Heaven.

Beat.

Larry   How long you been doing this?

Alice   Three months.

Larry   Straight after he left you?

Alice   No one left me.

Beat. **Larry** *glances round the room.*

Larry   Been here already tonight?
Alice   Yes.

Larry   With who?

Alice   A couple. A man and a woman.

Larry   What did you do?

Alice   I stripped, I danced, I bent over.

Larry   You gave this *couple* a thrill?

Alice   I think so.

Larry   What d'you talk about?

Alice   This and that.

Larry   D'you tell the truth?

Alice   Yes and no.

Larry   Are you telling *me* the truth?

Alice   Yes.

Larry   And no?

Alice   I'm telling you the truth.

Larry   Why?

Alice   Because it's what you want.

Larry   <u>Yes</u>. *It's what I <u>want</u>.*

He stares at her.

Nice *wig*.

Alice   Thank you.

Larry   Does it turn you on?

Alice   Sometimes.

Larry   *Liar.* You're telling me it turns you on because you think that's what I want to <u>hear</u>. You think *I'm* turned on by it turning *you* on.

Alice   The thought of me *creaming* myself when I strip for strangers doesn't turn you on?

Larry   Put like that . . . yes.

She shows him her behind.

Are you flirting with me?

Alice   Maybe.

Larry   Are you *allowed* to flirt with me?

Alice   Sure.

Larry   Really?

Alice   No I'm not, I'm breaking all the rules.

Larry   You're mocking me.

She sits opposite him.

Alice   Yes, I'm allowed to flirt.

Larry   To prise my money from me.

Alice   To prise your money from you I can say or do as I please.

Larry   Except *touch*.

Alice   We are not allowed to touch.

Larry   Is that a good rule do you think?

Alice   Sometimes.

Beat.

Larry   Open your legs.

She does so.

Wider.

She does so. Pause. **Larry** *looks between her legs.*

What would happen if I touched you now?

Alice   I would call Security.

Larry   And what would they do?

Alice   They would ask you to leave and ask you not to come back.

Larry   And if I refused to leave?

Alice   They would remove you. This is a two-way mirror.

She nods in the direction of the audience.

There are cameras in the ceiling.

Beat. **Larry** *glances up and to the audience.*

Larry   I think it's best that I don't attempt to touch you.

He looks at her.

I'd like to touch you . . . *later.*

Alice   I'm not a whore.

Larry   I wouldn't pay.

He gazes at her.

Why the fuck did he leave you?

Beat.

Alice   What's your job?

Larry   A question, you've asked me a question.

Alice   So?

Larry   It's a chink in your armour.

Alice   I'm not wearing armour.

Larry   *Yes you are.*
I'm in the skin trade.

Alice   You own strip clubs?

Larry (*smiles*)   Do I look like the sort of man who owns strip clubs?

Alice   Yes.

Larry *looks in the mirror / audience.*

Larry   Define that look.

Alice   *Rich.*

Larry   Close your legs. I don't own strip clubs.

Alice   Do you own golf clubs?

Larry   You know what I do.

He stands.

Why are you calling yourself Jane?

Alice   Because it's my name.

Larry   But we both know it isn't.
You're all protecting your identities. The girl in there who calls herself 'Venus'. What's her *real* name?

Alice   Pluto.

Larry   You're cheeky.

Alice   Would you like me to stop being cheeky?

Larry   No.

Beat.

Alice   What's *your* name?

Larry *considers.*

Larry   Daniel.

Beat.

Alice   Daniel the Dermatologist.

Larry   I never told you my job.

Alice   I guessed.

Larry *looks at her.*

Larry (*close*)   You're *strong.*

There's another one in there (judging by the scars, a recent patient of 'Doctor Tit'), she calls herself 'Cupid'. Who's going to tell her Cupid was a bloke?

Alice   He wasn't a bloke, he was a little boy.

Pause.

Larry   I'd like you to tell me your name. *Please.*

He gives her £20.

Alice   Thank you. My name is Jane.

Larry   Your *real* name.

He gives her £20.

Alice   Thank you. My real name is Jane.

Larry   Careful.

He gives her £20.

Alice   Thank you. It's still Jane.

Larry   I've got another five hundred quid here.

He takes out the money.

Why don't I give you – All – This – Money – and you tell me what your Real Name is,

He raises her face towards his with the wad of notes.

Alice.

She tries to take the money. **Larry** *withdraws it.*

Alice   I promise.

Larry *gives her the money.*

Alice   Thank you. My real name is Plain – Jane – Jones.

Larry   I may be rich but I'm not stupid.

Alice   What a shame, 'Doc', I love 'em rich and stupid.

Larry   DON'T FUCK AROUND WITH ME.

Alice   I apologise.

Larry   *Accepted.* All the girls in this hellhole; the pneumatic robots, the coked-up baby dolls – and you're no different – you all use 'stage names' to con yourselves you're someone else so you don't feel <u>ashamed</u> when you show your <u>cunts</u> and <u>arseholes</u> to Complete Fucking Strangers.

I'm trying to have a conversation here.

Alice   You're out of cash, Buster.

Larry   I've paid for the room.

Alice   This is extra.

Pause.

Larry   We met last year.

Alice   Wrong girl.

Larry   I touched your face at Anna's . . . opening.

I know you're in grief. I know you're . . . '*destroyed*'.

TALK TO ME.

Alice   I am.

Larry   Talk to me in <u>real life</u>.

I didn't know you'd be here.

I know who you are.

I love your scar, I love everything about you that hurts.

Silence. **Larry** *slowly breaks down.*

She won't even see me . . .

You feel the same, I *know* you feel the same.

Alice   You can't cry here.

Larry   Hold me, let me hold you.

Larry *approaches her.*

Alice   We're not allowed to touch.

Pause.

Larry   Come home with me, Alice. It's *safe*. Let me look after you.

Alice   I don't need looking after.

Larry   *Everyone* needs looking after.

Alice   I'm not your revenge fuck.

Pause.

Larry   I'll pay you.

Alice   I don't need your money.

Larry   You *have* my money.

Alice   Thank you.

Larry   THANK YOU, THANK YOU. Is that some kind of <u>rule</u>?

Alice   I'm just being polite.

Pause. **Larry** *sits down.*

Larry   Get a lot of men in here, crying their guts out?

Alice   Occupational hazard.

Beat.

Larry   Have you ever desired a customer?

Alice   Yes.

Larry   Put me out of my misery, do you . . . desire *me*? Because I'm being pretty fucking honest about my feelings for *you*.

Alice   Your '*feelings*'?

Larry   Whatever.

Beat.

Alice   No. I don't desire you.

Pause.

Larry   Thank you. Thank you sincerely for your honesty. Next question: do you think it's possible you could perceive me as something other than a sad slot machine spewing out money?

Alice   That's the transaction; you're the customer, I'm the service.

Larry   Hey, we're in a <u>strip club</u>, let's not debate sexual politics.

Alice   *Debate?*

Larry   You're asking for a smack, gorgeous.

Alice   No I'm not.

Beat.

Larry   But you *are* gorgeous.

Alice   'Thank you.'

Pause. **Larry** *stands, straightens his tie, lights a cigarette.*

Larry   Will you lend me my cab fare?

Alice (*laughing*)   No.

Larry   I'll give it back to you tomorrow . . .

Alice   Company policy, you give *us* the money.

Larry   And what do we get in return?

Alice   We're nice to you.

Larry   'And We Get To See You Naked.'

Alice   It's beautiful.

Larry   <u>Except</u> . . . you think you haven't given us anything of yourselves.

You think because you don't love us or desire us or even <u>like</u> us you think you've <u>won</u>.

Alice   It's not a war.

Larry *laughs for some time.*

Larry   But you <u>do</u> give us something of yourselves: you give us . . . *imagery* . . . and we do with it what we will.

If you women could see one minute of our Home Movies – the shit that slops through our minds every day – you'd string us up by our balls, you really would.

You don't understand the territory.
Because you *are* the territory.

I could tell you to strip right now . . .

Alice   Yes. Do you want me to?

Larry   No.

Alice . . . tell me something *true*.

Alice   Lying is the most fun a girl can have without taking her clothes off. But it's better if you do.

Larry   You're cold. You're all cold at heart.

He stares into the two-way mirror.

WHAT D'YOU HAVE TO DO TO GET A BIT OF INTIMACY AROUND HERE?

Alice   Well, maybe next time I'll have worked on my intimacy.

Larry   No. I'll tell you what's going to <u>work</u>. What's going to <u>work</u> is that you're going to take your clothes off right now and you're going to turn around *very slowly* and bend over and touch the fucking floor for my viewing pleasure.

Alice   That's what you want?

Beat.

Larry   What else could I want?

Blackout.

Scene Eight

Restaurant.

Evening/lunchtime. October (a month later).

Dan *is sitting at a table with a drink. He is smoking. He waits.*
Anna *joins him.*

Anna   Sorry, I'm really sorry.

Dan *kisses her.*

Dan   What happened?

Anna   Traffic.

Anna *sits.*

Dan   You're flushed, you didn't need to run.

Anna *smiles.*

Anna   Have you ordered?

Dan   I ordered a menu about ten years ago.

Pause. **Dan** *looks at her.*

So . . . how was it?

Anna   Oh . . . fine.

Beat.

Dan   You had lunch?

Anna   Mmhmm.

Beat.

Dan   Where?

Beat.

Anna   Here, actually.

Dan   *Here?*

Anna   He chose it.

Dan   Then what?

Anna   Then we left.

Pause.

Dan   *And?*

Anna   There is no 'and'.

Dan   You haven't seen him for four months, there must be an 'and'.

Anna *shrugs.*

Dan   How is he?

Anna   Terrible.

Dan   How's his *dermatology?*

Anna   He is now in private practice.

Dan   How does he square that with his politics?

Anna   He's not much concerned with politics at present.

Beat.

Dan   Was he weeping all over the place?

Anna   Some of the time.

Dan (*genuine*)   Poor bastard.

Was he . . . 'difficult' . . . ?

Anna   Are you angry I saw him?

Dan   No, no, it's just . . . I haven't seen *Alice.*

Anna   You <u>can't</u> see Alice, you don't know where she is.

Dan   I haven't tried to find her.

Anna   He's been begging me to see him for months, you *know* why I saw him, I saw him so he'd . . . <u>*sign*</u>.

Dan   So has he signed?

Anna   *Yes.*

Dan   Congratulations. You are now a divorcee – double divorcee. Sorry.

He takes her hand.

How do you feel?

Anna   Tired.

Dan *kisses her hand,* **Anna** *kisses his.*

Dan   I love you. *And* . . . I need a piss.

Dan *exits.*

Anna *reaches into her bag and pulls out the divorce papers.*

Larry *enters.*

Larry (*sitting*)   Afternoon.

Anna   Hi.

Larry *looks around.*

Larry   I hate this place.

Anna   At least it's central.

Larry   I hate central. The centre of London's a theme park. I hate 'retro' and I hate the future. Where does that leave me?

He looks at her.

Come back.

Anna   You promised you wouldn't.

Larry   *Come back.*

Beat.

Anna   How's work?

Larry   Oh, Jesus. Work's shit, OK.

He looks around for a waiter.

(*Loud.*) Do they <u>have</u> waiters here?

Anna   They're all busy.

Larry   I love you. Please come back.

Anna   I'm not coming back.

She spreads the divorce papers on the table. **Larry** *stares at them.*

Sign this, please.

Larry   No pen.

Anna *hands him her pen.*

Anna   Pen.

Larry *takes her hand.*

Anna   Give me back my hand . . .

Larry *lets go.*

Anna   Sign.

Beat.

Larry   I'll sign it on one condition: we skip lunch, we go to my sleek, little surgery and we christen the patients' bed with our final fuck. I know you don't *want* to, I know you think I'm *sick* for asking – but that's what I'm asking – 'For Old Times' Sake', because I'm obsessed with you, because I can't get over you unless you . . . because I think on some small level you owe me *something*, for deceiving me so . . . <u>*exquisitely*</u>.

For all these reasons I'm *begging* you to give me your body. Be my whore and in return I will pay you with your liberty. If you do this I swear I will not contact you again – you know I'm a man of my word.

I will divorce you and, in time, consider the possibility of a friendship.

He stands.

I'm going to the bar. I assume you still drink vodka tonic?

Anna *nods.*

Larry *exits.*

Dan *returns and sits.*

Dan   Any sign of a waiter?

Anna   No.

Dan   Do you want some food?

Anna   I'm not hungry.

Dan *stares at her,* **Anna** *turns to him, slowly.*

Dan   You slept with him, didn't you?

Pause.

Anna   Yes. I'm . . . 'sorry' . . .

Dan *smiles.*

Dan   What do you expect me to do?

Anna   Understand . . . hopefully?

Beat.

Dan   Why didn't you lie to me?

Anna   We said we'd always tell each other the truth.

Dan   What's so great about the truth? Try lying for a change – it's the currency of the world.

Anna   Dan, I did what he wanted and now he will <u>leave us alone</u>.
I love *you*, I didn't give *him* anything.

Dan   Your body?

Dan *reaches for his cigarettes.*

Anna   If Alice came to you . . . *desperate* . . . with all that
love still between you and she said she needed you to want
her so that she could get over you, you would do it. I
wouldn't like it either but I would forgive you because it's
. . . a mercy fuck – a *sympathy* fuck. Moral rape, everyone
does it. It's . . . *kindness*.

Dan   No, it's <u>cowardice</u>.
You don't have the guts to let him hate you.

Did you enjoy it?

Anna   *No.*

Dan   So you hated every second of it?

Anna *looks at* **Dan**.

Dan   Did you come?

Anna   No.

Dan   Did you fake it?

Anna   Yes.

Dan   Why?

Anna   To make him *think* I enjoyed it, why do you think?

Dan   If you were just his <u>*slag*</u> why did you give him the
pleasure of thinking you'd enjoyed it?

Anna   Because that's what slags *do*.

Dan   You fake it with me?

Anna   Yes, yes I do. I fake one in three, all right?

Dan   Tell me the truth.

Pause.

Anna   *Occasionally* . . . I have faked it.
It's not important, you don't *make* me come. I <u>come</u> . . .
you're . . . 'in the area' . . . providing valiant assistance.

Dan   You make *me* come.

Anna   You're a man, you'd come if the tooth fairy winked at you.

Beat.

Dan   You're late because you've come straight here from being with him.

Beat.

Anna   Yes.

Dan   Where was it?

Anna   His new surgery.

Beat.

Dan   Long session.

Anna *tries to touch him, he pulls away from her.*

Anna   Dan, please be bigger than . . . *jealous*. Please, be bigger.

Dan   What could be bigger than jealousy?

Long silence.

Anna   When we're making love, why don't you kiss me?
Why don't you like it when I say I love you?
I'm on your side. *Talk to me.*

Dan   It *hurts*. I'm ashamed. I know it's illogical and I do understand but *I hate you*.

I love you and I don't like other men <u>fucking</u> you, is that so weird?

Anna   No. YES. It was only <u>sex</u>.

Dan *(hard)*   If you can still fuck him you haven't left him.

(Softly.) It's gone . . . we're not innocent any more.

Anna   Don't stop loving me . . . I can see it draining out of you.
I'm sorry, it was a stupid thing to do. It meant *nothing*.
If you love me enough you'll forgive me.

Dan   Are you *testing* me?

Anna   *No.* Dan, I do understand.

Dan (*gently*)   No . . . *he* understands.

He looks at her.

All I can see is *him* all over you.

He's clever, your *ex*-husband . . . I almost admire him.

Silence.

Anna   Where are you?

Alice?

Dan (*smiles*)   I was reading the paper once. She wanted some attention. She crouched down on the carpet and pissed right in front of me.
Isn't that the most charming thing you've ever heard?

Anna (*tough*)   Why did you swear eternal love when all you wanted was a fuck?

Dan   I didn't just want a fuck, I wanted <u>you</u>.

Anna   You wanted excitement, love bores you.

Dan   No . . . it disappoints me.

I think you enjoyed it; he wheedles you into bed, the old jokes, the strange familiarity,
I think you had 'a whale of a time' and the truth is, I'll never know unless I ask <u>*him*</u>.

Anna   Well, why don't you?

Larry *returns to the table with two drinks. Vodka tonic for* **Anna**, *Scotch and dry for himself.*

Larry   Vodka tonic for the lady.

Anna (*to* **Larry**)   Drink your drink and then we'll go.

Larry *looks at her.*

Anna (*to* **Larry**)   I'm doing this because I feel guilty and because I pity you. You know that, don't you?

Larry   Yes.

Anna (*to* **Larry**)   Feel good about yourself?

Larry   No.

Larry *drinks.*

Dan (*to* **Anna**)   I'm sorry . . .

Anna (*to* **Dan**)   I didn't do it to hurt you. It's not all about *you.*

Dan (*to* **Anna**)   I know.
Let's go home . . .

Dan *and* **Anna** *kiss.*

I'll get us a cab.

Dan *exits.* **Larry** *sits.*

Larry   Will you tell him?

Anna   I don't know.

Larry (*helpful*)   Better to be truthful about this sort of thing . . .

Anna   Sign.

Beat.

Larry   I forgive you.

Anna   <u>Sign</u>.

Larry *signs.*

Blackout.

Scene Nine

Museum.

Afternoon. November (a month later).

A glass cabinet containing a life-size model of a Victorian child. A girl, dressed in rags. Behind her a model of a London street circa 1880s.

Alice *is alone. She is wearing a cashmere sweater. She is looking at the exhibit.*

She is holding a small package.

Larry *enters. He watches her.*

Larry   'Young Woman, London'.

Alice *turns.*

Larry   Hallo, gorgeous.

Alice   You're late, you old fart.

Larry   Sorry.

They kiss, warmly.

You minx.

He tugs the sweater.

Alice   'The sacred sweater', I'll give it back.

Larry   It suits you. Keep it.

Alice   Thank you.

She hands him the package.

Happy birthday.

Larry   Thank you.
I'm late because I walked through Postman's Park to get here . . . and I had a little look . . . at the memorial.

Alice   Oh.

Larry   Yeah . . . *oh.*

Larry *looks at the exhibit, smiles.*

Alice   Do you hate me?

Larry   No, I adore you.

Alice   Do we have to talk about it?

Larry   Not if you don't want to.

She kisses him.

Alice   Thank you. I've got a surprise for you.

Larry   You're full of them.

Alice *looks at* **Larry**'*s watch.*

Alice   Wait here.

Alice *exits.*
Larry *opens the package, looks inside, smiles.*

Anna *enters looking at her watch. She has a guide book, camera and a large brown envelope. She is wearing the shoes* **Larry** *gave her in Scene Six.*
She sees **Larry***. Stops.* **Larry** *looks up, sees her.*

Anna   What are *you* doing here?

Larry   I'm . . . lazing on a Sunday afternoon. You?

Anna   I'm meeting Alice.

Beat.

Larry   Who?

Anna   Dan's Alice – Dan's ex-Alice. She phoned me at the studio this morning . . . she wants her negatives . . .

Larry   . . . Right . . .

Beat.

Anna   You don't go to museums.

Larry   The evidence would suggest otherwise.

Beat.

Anna (*suspicious*)   Are you OK?

Larry   Yeah, you?

Anna   Fine. It's your birthday today.

Larry   I know.

Beat.

Anna   I thought of you this morning.

Larry   Lucky me.

Beat.

Anna   Happy birthday.

Larry   Thank you.

Anna *nods to the package.*

Anna   Present?

Larry (*evasive*)   . . . *Yeah* . . .

Anna   What is it?

Larry   A Newton's Cradle.

Anna   Who from?

Beat.

Larry   My dad.

Anna   From *Joe*?

Pause.

Larry   It's from *Alice.*

I'm fucking her.

I – Am – Fucking – Alice.

She's set us up, I had no idea you were meeting her.

Pause.

Anna   You're old enough to be her ancestor.

Larry   Disgusting, isn't it.

Anna   You should be ashamed.

Larry (*smiles*)   Oh, I am.

Beat.

Anna   . . . *How?*

Larry (*vague*)   I went to a club, she happened to be there.

Anna   A *club?*

Larry   Yeah, a club.

Anna   You don't go to clubs.

Larry   I'm reliving my youth.

Anna   Was it a strip club?

Larry   You know, I can't remember.

He looks at **Anna**.

Jealous?

Anna *shrugs.*

Larry   Ah, well.

Anna   When did it start?

Larry   About a month ago.

Anna   <u>Before</u> or <u>after</u> I came to your surgery?

Larry   The night before. (*Dirty.*) She made me strip for
her.

Anna   I don't want to know.

Larry   I know.

Did you tell your 'soulmate' about *that* afternoon?

Anna   Of course.

Larry   How did he take it?

Beat.

Anna   Like a _man_.

She looks at him.

Larry   I told you it was best to be truthful.

Anna   You're sly.

Larry   Am I?

(*Fondly.*) You love your guide books, you look like a tourist.

Anna   I feel like one. Please don't hate me.

Larry   It's easier than loving you.

He looks at **Anna**.

Me and Alice . . . it's *nothing*.

Anna   Nice nothing?

Larry   Very.

They look at each other, close.

Since we're talking, could you have a word with your lawyer?
I'm still waiting for confirmation of our divorce.
If that's what you want.

Alice *enters.*

Alice   Hi, do you two know each other?

Larry   I think I'll leave you to it.

Alice   Good idea, we don't want *him* here while we're working, do we?

Larry (*to* **Alice**)   Later, Minx.
(*To* **Anna**.) Bye.

He makes to exit, turns.

(*To* **Anna**.) Nice shoes by the way.

Larry *exits.*

Anna   How did you get so brutal?

Alice   I lived a little.

Alice *strokes the sweater,* **Anna** *watches her.*

Anna   You're primitive.

Alice   Yeah, I am. How's Dan?

Anna   Fine.

Alice   Did you tell him you were seeing me?

Anna   No.

Alice   Do you cut off his crusts?

Anna   What?

Alice   Do you cut off his crusts?

Anna   What do you want?

Alice   I want my negatives.

Anna *hands the envelope to* **Alice**.

Alice   What's your latest project, Anna?

Anna   Derelict buildings.

Alice   How nice, the beauty of ugliness.

Anna   What are you doing with Larry?

Alice   *Everything.*

I like your bed.

You should come round one night, come and watch your husband blubbering into his pillow – it might help you develop a conscience.

Anna   I know what I've done.

Alice   His big thing at the moment is how upset his family are. Apparently, they all worship you, they can't understand why you had to ruin everything. He spends *hours* staring up my <u>arsehole</u> like there's going to be some answer there. Any ideas, Anna?

Why don't you go back to him?

Anna   And then Dan would go back to you?

Alice   Maybe.

Anna   *Ask* him.

Alice   I'm not a beggar.

Anna   Dan left you, I didn't force him to go.

Alice   You made yourself available, don't weasel out of it.

Anna   Screwing Larry was a big mistake.

Alice   Yeah, well, *everyone* screws Larry round here.

Anna   You're Dan's little girl, he won't like it.

Alice   <u>So don't tell him</u>, I think you owe me that.

Anna *looks away*.

Alice   She even looks beautiful when she's angry. The Perfect Woman.

Anna   JUST FUCKING STOP IT.

Alice   Now we're talking.

Anna   Why *now*, why come for me *now*?

Alice   Because I felt strong enough, it's taken me five months to convince myself you're not better than me.

Anna   It's not a competition.

Alice   <u>Yes it is</u>.

Anna   I don't want a fight.

Alice   SO GIVE IN.

Silence. They look at each other.

(*Gently.*) Why did you do this?

Anna (*tough*)   I fell in love with him, Alice.

Alice   That's the most stupid expression in the world.
'I fell in love' – as if you had no *choice*.
There's a moment, there's always a *moment*; I can do this, I can give in to this or I can resist it. I don't know when your moment was but I bet there was one.

Anna   Yes, there was.

Alice   You didn't fall in love, you gave in to temptation.

Anna   Well, *you* fell in love with him.

Alice   No, I *chose* him. I looked in his briefcase and I found this . . . *sandwich* . . . and I thought, 'I will give all my love to this charming man who cuts off his crusts.' I didn't *fall* in love, I chose to.

Anna   You still want him, after everything he's done to you?

Alice   You wouldn't understand, he . . . *buries* me.
He makes me invisible.

Anna (*curious*)   What are you *hiding* from?

Alice (*softly*)   Everything. Everything's a lie, nothing matters.

Anna   Too easy, Alice. It's the cop-out of the age.

Alice   Yeah, well, you're *old*.

Anna *smiles to herself, looks at* **Alice**.

Anna   I am sorry. I had a choice and I chose to be selfish.
I'm sorry.

Alice (*shrugs*)   Everyone's selfish, I stole Dan from someone else.

Anna   *Ruth?*

Alice   Ruth. She went to pieces when he left her.

Anna   Did *she* ever come and see *you*?

Alice   No.

She turns to **Anna**.

So . . . what are you going to do?

Anna   *Think.*

She touches **Alice**'s *sweater*.

Is Larry nice to you, in bed?

Alice   OK, Dan's better.

Anna   Rubbish, at least Larry's *there*.

Alice   Dan's there, in his own quiet way.

Anna   They spend a lifetime fucking and never know how to make love.

Pause.

Alice   I've got a scar on my leg, Larry's mad about it, he licks it like a dog. Any ideas?

Anna (*shrugs*)   *Dermatology*? God knows. This is what we're dealing with.

We arrive with our . . . 'baggage' and for a while they're brilliant, they're 'Baggage Handlers'.
We say, 'Where's *your* baggage?' They deny all knowledge of it . . . '*They're in love*' . . . they have none.
Then . . . just as you're relaxing . . . a Great Big Juggernaut arrives . . . with *their* baggage.
It Got Held Up.

They love the way we make them *feel* but not 'us'.
They love dreams.

Alice   So do we. You should lower your expectations.

Anna   It's easy to say that. I'm not being patronising but you're a child.

Alice   You are being patronising.

Anna   And you *are* a child.

They look at each other.

Who's '*Buster*'?

Alice   'Buster'? No idea.

Anna   He says it in his sleep.

Alice (*smiles*)   I've got to go.

Alice *makes to exit.*

Anna   Don't forget your negatives.

Alice *picks up the envelope.*

Alice   Oh, yeah. Thanks.

She hands the envelope to **Anna**.

Do the right thing, Anna.

Alice *exits.* **Anna** *looks at the envelope.*

Blackout.

Scene Ten

Larry's *surgery.*

Late afternoon. December (a month later).

On **Larry**'s *desk: computer, phone, a Newton's Cradle. Also in the room, a surgery bed.* **Larry** *is seated at his desk.*
Dan *is standing, distraught. He holds his brown briefcase.*

Silence.

Larry   So?

Dan   I want Anna back.

Larry   She's made her choice.
You look like *shit*.

Beat. **Dan** *puts his briefcase down.*

Dan   I owe you an apology. I fell in love with her.
My intention was not to make you suffer.

Larry   Where's the apology? You <u>cunt</u>.

Dan   I apologise.

If you love her, you'll let her go so she can be . . . happy.

Larry   She doesn't want to be 'happy'.

Dan   Everyone wants to be happy.

Larry   Depressives don't. They want to be *unhappy* to
confirm they're depressed. If they were <u>happy</u> they couldn't
be depressed any more, they'd have to go out into the world
and <u>*live*</u>, which can be . . . *depressing*.

Dan   Anna's not a depressive.

Larry   Isn't she?

Dan   I love her.

Larry   Boo hoo, so do I. You don't love Anna, you love
yourself.

Dan   You're *wrong*, <u>I don't love myself</u>.

Larry   Yes you do, and you know something; you're
winning – you selfish people – it's *your* world. <u>*Nice*</u>, isn't it?

Dan *glances round the sleek surgery.*

Dan   *Nice* office.
It's *you* who's selfish. You don't even want *Anna*, you want
<u>revenge</u>.

She's gone back to you because she can't bear your *suffering*. You don't know who she is, you love her like a dog loves its owner.

Larry   And the owner loves the dog for so doing. Companionship will always triumph over '*passion*'.

Dan   You'll hurt her, you'll never forgive her.

Larry   Of course I'll forgive her – I *have* forgiven her. Without forgiveness we're savages. You're <u>*drowning*</u>.

Dan   You only *met* her because of me.

Larry   Yeah . . . *thanks.*

Dan   It's a joke, your marriage to her is a <u>joke</u>.

Larry   Here's a good one: she never sent the divorce papers to her lawyer.

To a 'Towering Romantic Hero' like you I don't doubt I'm somewhat common but I am, nevertheless, what she has chosen.

And we must respect What The Woman Wants.

If you go *near* her again, I promise –

The phone rings.

– I will kill you.

He picks it up.

(*In phone.*) Uh-huh. OK.

He puts the phone down.

I have patients to see.

He takes his jacket off to prepare for his patient.

Dan   When she came here you think she enjoyed it?

Larry   I didn't fuck her to give her a '*nice time*'. I fucked her to fuck you up. A good fight is never clean.

And yeah, she enjoyed it, as you know, she loves a guilty fuck.

Dan   You're an animal.

Larry   YES. What are _you_?

Dan   You think love is simple? You think the heart is like a diagram?

Larry   Ever _seen_ a human heart? It looks like a fist wrapped in blood.
GO FUCK YOURSELF . . . you . . . _WRITER_. You LIAR. Go check a few facts while I get my hands dirty.

Dan   She hates your hands. She hates your simplicity.

Pause.

Larry   Listen . . . I've spent the whole week talking about _you_.

Anna tells me you fucked her with your eyes closed.
She tells me you wake in the night, crying for your dead mother.

You mummy's boy.

Shall we stop this?

It's _over_. Accept it.

You don't know the first thing about love because you don't understand _compromise_.

You don't even know . . . _Alice_.

Dan _looks at him._

Larry   Consider her scar, how did she get that?
Beat.

Dan   When did _you_ meet Alice?

Pause.

Larry   Anna's exhibition. _You_ remember.

A scar in the shape of a question mark, solve the mystery.

Dan   She got it when her parents' car crashed.

Pause.

Larry   There's a condition called '*dermatitis artefacta*'. It's a mental disorder manifested in the skin. The patient manufactures his or her very own skin disease. They pour bleach on themselves, gouge their skin, inject themselves with their own piss, sometimes their own shit. They create their own disease with the same diabolical attention to detail as the artist or the lover. It looks 'real' but its source is the deluded self.

He takes a roll of paper and makes a new sheet on the surgery bed.

I think Alice mutilated herself.
It's fairly common in children who lose their parents young. They blame themselves, they're disturbed.

Dan   Alice is not 'disturbed'.

Larry   But she <u>*is*</u>.
You were so busy feeling your grand artistic '*feelings*' you couldn't see what was in front of you. The girl is fragile and tender. She didn't want to be put in a book, she wanted to be *loved*.

Dan   How do *you* know?

Beat.

Larry   Clinical observation.

*He hands **Dan** his briefcase indicating for him to leave.*
*He looks at **Dan**, close.*

Don't cry on me.

*Silence. **Dan** breaks down, uncontrollably. **Larry** observes him.*

Dan   I'm sorry.

He continues to cry.

I don't know what to do.

Larry *watches him sob. Eventually . . .*

Larry   Sit down.

Dan *sinks into a chair, head in hands.*

Larry   You want my advice? Go back to her.

Dan   She'd never have me. She's vanished.

Pause.

Larry   No, she hasn't.

Dan *looks up.*

Larry   I found her . . . by accident. She's working in . . . a
. . . 'club'.
Yes, I saw her naked.
No, I did not fuck her.

Dan   You spoke to her?

Larry   Yes.

Dan   What about?

Larry   *You.*

The phone rings. **Larry** *picks it up. He hands* **Dan** *a Kleenex.*

(*In phone.*) Yes. One minute.

Larry *puts the phone down. He writes on his prescription pad.*

Dan   How is she?

Larry (*writing*)   She loves you. Beyond Comprehension.
Here . . . your prescription.

He hands **Dan** *a piece of paper.*

It's where she works.

<u>Go to her</u>.

They look at each other.

Dan   Thank you.

Larry *starts to consult his files.*
Dan *moves to leave but then gestures to the Newton's Cradle.*

Dan   Where did you get that?

Larry   A present.

He begins to work on his computer.

Still pissing about on the Net?

Dan   Not recently.

Beat.

Larry   I wanted to *kill* you.

Dan   I thought you wanted to *fuck* me.

Larry (*smiles*)   Don't get lippy.
I liked your book by the way.

Dan   Thanks . . . You Stand Alone.

Larry   *With Anna.*

You should write another one.

Dan (*shrugs*)   Haven't got a subject.

Beat.

Larry   When I was nine, a policeman touched me up.
He was my uncle. Still *is*. <u>Uncle Ted</u>.
Nice bloke, married, bit of a demon darts player.

Don't tell me you haven't got a subject, every human life is
a million stories.

Thank God life *ends* – we'd never survive it.

From Big Bang to weary shag, the history of the world.

Our flesh is ferocious . . . our bodies will kill us . . . our
bones will outlive us.

Still writing obituaries?

Dan   Yes.

Larry   Busy?

Dan (*nods*)   I was made editor.

Larry   Yeah? How come?

Dan   The previous editor died.

They smile.

Alcohol poisoning. I sat with him for a week, in the hospital.

They look at each other.

Larry   I really do have patients to see.

Dan *gestures to the Newton's Cradle.*

Dan   Alice . . . gave me one of those.

Larry   Really?

Beat.

Dan   And yours?

Larry   My dad.

Dan (*suspicious*)   Your father?

Larry   Yeah, he loves old tat.

Dan   He's a cab driver, isn't he?

Larry   Yeah.

*He points to **Dan** indicating, 'and yours'.*

. . . Teacher?

Dan   History.

Pause. **Larry** *sets the cradle in motion. They watch it moving.*

Larry   You should never have messed with Anna.

Dan *gets up.*

Dan   I know, I'm sorry. Thank you.

Larry For what?

Dan Being kind.

Larry I am kind. Your invoice is in the post.

Dan *goes to exit.*

Larry Dan . . .

Dan *turns to* **Larry**.

Larry I lied to you.

I did fuck Alice.

I'm sorry for telling you.

I'm just . . . not . . . *big enough* to forgive you.

Buster.

They look at each other.

Blackout.

Scene Eleven

Hotel room.

Late night. January (a month later).

Dan *is lying on the bed, smoking. He is reading a Gideon's Bible. He stubs his cigarette in the ashtray.*
Alice *is in the bathroom offstage.*

Alice (*off*) SHOW ME THE SNEER.

Dan *sneers in the direction of the bathroom.*

Alice (*off*) BOLLOCKS.

Dan (*laughing*) It's two in the morning, you'll wake the hotel.

Alice *enters in her pyjamas. She cartwheels on to the bed.*

Alice   Fuck me!

Dan   *Again*? We have to be up at six.

Alice   How can *one* man be so endlessly disappointing?

Dan   That's my *charm*.

Alice *lies in his arms.*

Dan   So . . . where are we going?

Alice   My treat – my holiday surprise – my rules.

Dan *tickles her.*

Dan   <u>*Where*</u> are we *going*?

Alice (*laughing*)   New York.

Dan   You angel.
How long's the flight?

Alice   Seven hours.

Dan   I can't fly for seven hours.

Alice   The *plane* will do the flying. I'll protect you.

She kisses him.

Don't be scared of flying.

Dan   I'm not, I'm scared of *crashing*. Did you remember to pack my passport?

Alice   Of course, it's with my passport.

Dan   And where's that?

Alice   In a place where *you* can't look. *No one* sees my passport photo.

Dan *strokes her.*

Alice   Hey, when we get on the plane we'll have been together four years.
Happy anniversary . . . *Buster*.

Dan *stops, looks at her.*

Dan   I'm going to take my eyes out.

Alice   Brush your teeth as well.

Dan *gets off the bed.*

Dan   What was in my sandwiches?

Alice   Tuna.

Dan   What colour was my apple?

Alice   Green.

Dan   It was *red*.

Alice   It was *green* and it was horrible.

Dan   What were your first words to me?

Alice   'Hallo, Stranger.'

Dan   What a slut.

Beat.

Alice   Where had I been?

Dan   'Clubbing', then the meat market and then . . . the buried river.

Beat.

Alice   The what?

Dan   You went to Blackfriars Bridge to see where the Fleet river comes out . . . *the swimming pig* . . . all that.

Alice   You've lost the plot, *Grandad*.

Dan *'remembers' and exits to the bathroom.*

Dan *(off)*   And you went to that park . . . with the memorial.

Alice   Who did *you* go there with?

Dan *(off)*   My old dead dad.

Alice   He ate an egg sandwich, he had butter on his chin.

Dan (*off*)   How do you *remember* these things?

Alice   Because *my* head's not full of specky, egghead <u>rubbish</u>.
What was your euphemism?

Dan (*off*)   Reserved. Yours?

Alice   Disarming. Were the chairs red or yellow?

Dan *enters. He is now wearing his spectacles.*

Dan   No idea.

Alice   Trick question, they were orange.

Dan   *You* are a trick question. *Damsel.*

Alice   *Knight.*

Alice *opens her legs.* **Dan** *looks at her, remembers something.*

Pause.

Dan   Do you remember a doctor?

Beat.

Alice   No . . . what doctor?

Pause.

Dan   There was a *doctor* . . . he gave you a cigarette.

Beat.

Alice   No. I haven't been on holiday for . . . *ever.*

Dan   We went to the country.

Alice   That doesn't count, you were making sneaky calls to that . . . *witch* we do not mention.

Dan *watches her.*

Dan   Do you think they're happy?

Alice   Who?

Dan   Anna and . . . *Larry*.

Alice   Couldn't give a toss. Come to bed.

Dan   I want a *fag*. How did *you* manage to give up?

Alice   Deep Inner Strength.

Dan *gets into bed. He holds* **Alice**, *kisses her, strokes her leg.*

Dan   How *did* you get this?

Alice   You know how.

Dan   How?

Alice   I fell off my bike because I refused to use stabilisers.

Dan (*disbelieving*)   Really?

Alice   You know how I got it.

Beat.

Dan   Did you do it yourself?

Alice   No.

Beat.

Dan   Show me your passport.

Alice   No, I look ugly.

Beat.

Dan   When are you going to stop stripping?

Alice   Soon.

Dan   You're *addicted* to it.

Alice   No I'm not.

It paid for this.

Pause. **Dan** *struggles but can't stop himself.*

Dan   Tell me what happened.

Alice   Dan . . . *don't*. Nothing happened.

Dan   But he came to the club?

Alice   Loads of men came to the club. *You* came to the club. The look on your face.

Dan   The look on *your* face.
What a face. What a *wig*.

He gazes at her.

I *love* your face . . . I saw *this* face . . . this . . . *vision*.
And then you stepped into the road.
It was the moment of my life.

Alice   *This* is the moment of your life.

Dan   You were perfect.

Alice   I still am.

Dan   I know.

On the way to the hospital . . . when you were '*lolling*' . . . I kissed your forehead.

Alice   You brute!

Dan   The cabbie saw me kiss you . . . he said, 'Is she yours?' and I said, 'Yes . . . she's *mine*.'

He kisses her forehead, holds her close. Struggles with himself.

So he came to the club, watched you strip, had a little chat and that was it?

Alice   Yes.

Dan   You're not *trusting* me. I'm in love with you, you're *safe*. If you fucked him you fucked him, I just <u>want to know</u>.

Alice   Why?

Dan (*tenderly*)   Because I want to know *everything* because . . . I'm . . . *insane*.

He strokes her face. Pause.

<u>*Tell me*</u> . . .

Long silence.

Alice   Nothing happened. You were living with someone else.

Dan (*sharp*)   What are you justifying?

Alice   I'm not justifying anything . . . I'm just *saying*.

Dan   What are you <u>saying</u>?

Alice   I'm not saying anything.

Dan   <u>I just want the truth</u>.

Dan *gets out of bed and puts his trousers on.*

Alice   I'm telling you the truth.

Dan   You and the truth are known strangers.

Did you ever give him a present?

Beat.

Alice   No. Where are you going?

Dan   Cigarettes.

Alice   Everywhere's closed.

Dan   I'll go to the terminal, I'll be back soon.

He puts his coat on.

When I get back *please* tell me the truth.

Alice   Why?

Dan   Because I'm addicted to it. Because without it we're animals. Trust me, I love you.

He looks at her.

What?

Alice *slowly turns to him.*

Silence.

Alice   I don't love you any more.

Pause.

Dan   Look . . . I'm sorry . . .

Alice   No, I've changed the subject. I don't love you any more.

Dan   Since when?

Alice (*gently*)   Now . . . Just Now.

I don't want to lie and I can't tell the truth so it's over.

Dan   Alice . . . don't leave me.

Alice *gets out of bed and goes to her rucksack, she finds* **Dan***'s passport and hands it to him.*

Alice   I've left . . . I've *gone*.
'I don't love you any more. Goodbye.'

Beat.

Dan   Why don't you tell me the truth?

Alice (*softly*)   So you can hate me?
I fucked Larry. Many times. I enjoyed it. I came. I prefer *you*. Now go.

Pause.

Dan   I knew that, he told me.

Alice   You *knew*?

Dan   I needed *you* to tell me.

Alice   *Why?*

Dan   Because he might've been lying, I had to hear it from *you*.

Alice   I would never have told you because I know you'd never forgive me.

Dan   I would, I *have*!

Alice   Why did he tell you?

Dan   Because he's a <u>bastard</u>!

Alice (*distraught*)   How could he?

Dan   Because he wanted <u>this</u> to happen.

Alice   But why *test* me?

Dan   <u>Because I'm an idiot.</u>

Alice   *Yeah.*

I would've loved you for ever. Now, please go.

Dan   Don't do this, Alice, talk to me.

Alice   I'm talking – *fuck off.*

Dan   I'm sorry, you misunderstand, I didn't mean to –

Alice   Yes you did.

Dan   *I love you.*

Alice   *<u>Where</u>?*

Dan   What?

Alice   *Show me.* Where is this '*<u>love</u>*'?
I can't see it, I can't *touch* it, I can't *feel* it.
I can <u>hear</u> it, I can hear some *<u>words</u>* but I can't *do* anything
with your easy words.

Dan   Listen to me, please –

Alice   Whatever you say it's too late.

Dan (*desperately*)   *Please* don't do this.

Alice   <u>It's done</u>. Now <u>go</u> or I'll call . . . *security.*

Beat.

Dan   You're not in a strip club. There is no security.

They look at each other. Pause.

Alice *tries to grab the phone.* **Dan** *throws her on to the bed. They struggle.*

Dan   Why d'you fuck him?

Alice   I wanted to.

Dan   *Why?*

Alice   I <u>desired</u> him.

Dan   <u>*Why?*</u>

Alice   *You* weren't there.

Dan   Why <u>him</u>?

Alice   He asked me nicely.

Dan   <u>You're a liar</u>.

Alice   So?

Dan   WHO ARE YOU?

Alice   I'M NO ONE.

She spits in his face. He grabs her by the throat, one hand.

Alice   Go on, hit me. That's what you *want*. <u>Hit me, you fucker</u>.

Silence.

Dan *hits* **Alice**, *a slap across her face.*

Silence.

Alice   Do you have a single original thought in your head?

Blackout.

Scene Twelve

Postman's Park.

Afternoon. July (six months later).

A summer's day. **Anna** *is looking at the memorial. She has a guide book.*
Larry *stands, holding his white coat. He carries two styrofoam cups. He watches her. She turns.*

Anna   *Spy.*

Larry *approaches.*

Anna   You've got the coat.

Larry   The white coat.

Anna   Hallo, Doctor Larry.

Larry *hands a cup to* **Anna**.

Anna   Thanks. Have you read these?

Anna *turns back to the memorial.*

Larry   Yeah, I knew you'd like it.

Larry *sits on a park bench and lights a cigarette.*

Anna (*reading*)   'Elizabeth Boxall . . . aged seventeen . . .
who died of injuries received in trying to save a child from a
runaway horse. June 20th 1888.'

She turns to **Larry**.

How's Polly?

Beat.

Larry   Polly's great.

Anna   I always knew you'd end up with a pretty nurse.

Larry   Yeah? How?

Anna   I just thought you would.

Is she . . . 'the one'?

Larry   I don't know.

He glances at **Anna**.

No.

Everyone learns, nobody changes.

Anna   *You* don't change.

Beat.

Larry   You . . . seeing anyone?

Anna   No.

I got a dog.

Larry   Yeah? What sort?

Anna   Mongrel, she's a stray. I found her in the street, no collar . . . nothing.

Pause.

Larry   You look fantastic.

Anna   Don't *start*.

Larry   I'd give you one . . .

Anna *looks at him.*

Larry   Serious.

Anna   Fuck off and die, you fucked-up slag.

Pause.

Larry   I never told you this: when I strode into the bathroom . . . *that night* . . . I banged my knee on our cast-iron tub. The bathroom *ambushed* me. While you were sobbing in the sitting room I was hopping around in agony. The mirror was having a field day.

Anna *smiles.*

Larry   How's work?

Anna   I'm having a break . . . I'm taking the dog to the country . . . we're going to go for long walks.

Beat.

Larry   Don't become . . . a sad person.

Anna   I won't. I'm *not*. <u>Fuck off</u>.

Larry *looks at her.*

Larry   Don't give your love to a dog.

Anna   Well, *you* didn't want it, in the end.

There's always someone younger.

They look out at the memorial.

Silence.

Larry   How did she die?

Anna   I don't know. When he phoned, he said it
happened last night in New York.
He's flying out today and he wanted to see us before he left.

Larry   So they weren't together?

Anna   They split up in January.

Beat.

Larry   Did he say why?

Anna   No.

Beat.

Larry   How did they contact him?

Anna   Maybe she wrote his name in her passport as 'next
of kin'.
You're still in mine – 'in the event of death'.
I must remove you.

Are you glad you're back at the hospital?

She sits with **Larry**.

Larry   Yeah. Well, Polly said she wouldn't have sex with
me until I gave up private medicine. What's a man to do?

Anna *looks at the memorial.*

Anna   Do you think the families arranged these?

Larry   I suppose. It's like putting flowers at the roadside.
People need to remember.
It makes things seem less . . . random.

Actually, I hate this memorial.

Anna   Why?

Larry   It's the sentimental act of a Victorian
philanthropist: remember the dead, forget the living.

Anna   You're a pompous bastard.

Larry   And *you* are an incurable romantic.

Have a look for Alice Ayres.

Anna   Larry, that's horrible.

Larry *points to one memorial in particular.*

Larry (*reading*)   'Alice Ayres, daughter of a bricklayer's
labourer, who by intrepid conduct saved three children
from a burning house in Union Street, Borough, at the cost
of her own young life.

April 24th 1885.'

She made herself up.

They look at the memorial.
After a while, **Larry** *puts his cigarette out and picks up his white
coat.*

I'm not being callous but I've got a lot of patients to see.
Will you give my apologies to Dan? I'm not good at grief.

Anna   You're a coward.

Larry   I know.

Anna *continues to look at the memorial then turns to* **Larry**.

Anna   You do remember me?

They look at each other.

Dan *enters. He is wearing the suit and carrying the suitcase seen in Scene Five. He is holding a bunch of flowers. He is exhausted.*

Dan   I couldn't get away from work, sorry.

Larry   Dan . . . I'm sorry . . . I have to . . .

Dan   It's fine.

Larry *exits.*

Dan (*to* **Anna**)   You look well.

Anna   I am well.

Dan *looks out at the memorial.*

Anna   Dan . . .

Anna *gestures for him to sit, he remains standing.*

Dan   This is where we sat.

Anna   Who?

Dan   Me and my father, didn't I tell you?

Anna   No, wrong girl, you told Alice.

Beat.

Dan   *Jane.* Her name was Jane Jones.

The police phoned me . . . they said that someone I knew, called Jane, had died . . . (they found her address book).

I said there must be a mistake . . .

They had to *describe* her.

There's no one else to identify the body.

She was knocked down by a car . . . on Forty-third and Madison.

When I went to work today . . . Graham said, 'Who's on the slab?'

I went out to the fire escape and just . . . cried like a baby.

I covered my face – why do we do that?

A man from the Treasury had died.
I spent all morning . . . writing his obituary.

There's no space. There's not enough . . . *space*.

He sits on the bench with **Anna**.

The phone rang. It was the police . . . they said there's no
record of her parents' death . . . they said they were trying
to trace them.

She told me that she fell in love with me because . . . I cut
off my crusts . . . but it was just . . . it was only *that* day . . .
because the bread . . . *broke* in my hands.

He turns away from **Anna**, *looks at the flowers*.

Silence.

He turns back to **Anna**.

I bumped into *Ruth*.

She's married. One kid, another on the way.

She married . . . a Spanish *poet*.

He grimaces.

She translated his work and fell in love with him.

Fell in love with a collection of poems.

They were called . . . '*Solitude*'.

He holds on to the flowers.

I have to put these at Blackfriars Bridge.

Dan *and* **Anna** *stand*.

I have to go, I'll miss the plane.

They look at each other.

Goodbye.

Anna   Yes. Goodbye.

They exit separately.

Empty stage.

Blackout.

Appendix to Scene Three

In a production of *Closer* where budget or theatre sightlines won't allow for a projected version of this scene it may be possible for the actors to speak their lines whilst 'typing'. Permission, in this respect, must be sought from the author's agent when applying for the rights for the production.

The following dialogue may be used:

Scene Three

Early evening. January (the following year).

Dan *is in his flat sitting at a table with a computer. There is a Newton's Cradle on the table. Writerly sloth, etc.*

Larry *is sitting at his hospital desk with a computer. He is wearing a white coat.*

They are in separate rooms.

*They speak their 'dialogue' simultaneous to their typing it. The actors should speak word by word, almost robotically, as if they were dictating the words on to the screen, thus making a distinction between 'typed' speech and 'spoken' speech (e.g. **Larry** on the phone).*

Dan   Hallo.

Larry   Hi.

Dan   How are you?

Larry   OK.

Dan   Cum here often?

Larry   First time.

Dan   A Virgin. Welcome. What's your name?

Larry   Larry. You?

Dan *considers.*

Dan   Anna.

Larry   Nice to meet you.

Dan   I love COCK.

Pause.

Larry   You're v. forward.

Dan   And you are chatting on 'LONDON FUCK'. Do you want sex?

Larry   Yes. Describe you.

Dan   Dark hair. Dirty mouth. Epic Tits.

Larry   Define Epic.

Dan   Thirty-six double D.

Larry   Nice arse?

Dan   Y.

Larry   Because I want to know.

Dan *smiles.*

Dan   No, 'Y' means 'Yes'.

Larry   Oh.

Dan   I want to suck you senseless.

Larry   Be my guest.

Dan   Sit on my face, Fuckboy.

Larry   I'm there.

Dan   Wear my wet knickers.

Beat.

Larry   OK.

Dan   Are you well hung?

Larry   Nine pounds.

Larry (*speaking*)   Shit.

Larry (*typing*)   Nine inches.

Dan   GET IT OUT.

Larry *considers and then unzips. He puts his hand in his trousers. The phone on his desk rings. Loud. He jumps.*

Larry (*speaking*)   Wait.

Larry (*typing*)   wait.

Larry *picks up the phone.* **Dan** *lights a cigarette.*

Larry (*speaking*)   <u>Yes</u>. What's the histology? *Progressive?* Sounds like an atrophy.

Larry *puts the phone down and goes back to his keyboard.* **Dan** *clicks the balls on his Newton's Cradle.*

Larry   Hallo?

Dan *looks at his screen.*

Larry   Anna.

Larry (*speaking*)   Bollocks.

Larry (*typing*)   ANNA? WHERE ARE YOU?

Dan   Hey, big Larry, what do you wank about?

Larry *considers.*

Larry   Ex-girlfriends.

Dan   Not current g-friends?

Larry   Never.

Dan *smiles.*

Dan   Tell me your sex-ex fantasy . . .

Larry   Hotel room . . . they tie me up . . . tease me . . . won't let me come. They fight over me, six tongues on my cock, balls, perineum, et cetera.

Dan   All hail the Sultan of Twat?

Larry *laughs.*

Larry   Anna, what do you wank about?

Dan *thinks.*

Dan   Strangers.

Larry   Details.

Dan   They form a queue and I attend to them like a cum hungry bitch, one in each hole and both hands.

Larry   Then?

Dan   They come in my mouth arse tits cunt hair.

Larry (*speaking*)   Jesus.

Larry's *phone rings. He picks up the receiver and replaces it without answering. Then he takes it off the hook.*

Larry (*typing*)   Then?

Dan   I lick it off like the dirty slut I am. Wait, have to type with one hand . . . I'm coming right now . . . oh oh oh oh oh oh oh oh oh oh oh oh oh oh.

Pause. **Larry**, *motionless, stares at his screen.*

Larry   Was it good?

Dan   No.

Larry *shakes his head.*

Larry   I'm shocked.

Dan   PARADISE SHOULD BE SHOCKING.

Larry   Are you for real?

Beat.

Dan   MEET ME.

Pause.

Larry Serious?

Dan Yes.

Larry When.

Dan NOW.

Larry Can't. I'm a doctor. Must do rounds.

Dan *smiles.* **Larry** *flicks through his desk diary.*

Dan Don't be a pussy. Life without risk is death. Desire, like the world, is an accident. The best sex is anonymous. We live as we dream, ALONE. I'll make you come like a train.

Larry Tomorrow, one p.m., where?

Dan *thinks.*

Dan The Aquarium, London Zoo, and then HOTEL.

Larry How will you know me?

Dan Bring white coat.

Larry Eh?

Dan Doctor plus coat equals horn for me.

Larry OK.

Dan I send you a rose my love.

Larry Thanks. See you at Aquarium. Bye, Anna.

Dan Bye, Larry, kiss kiss kiss kiss kiss.

Larry Kiss kiss kiss kiss kiss kiss.

They look at their screens.

Blackout.

Notes

page
8 *Blackfriars Bridge*: bridge over the Thames in east London.

9 *Smithfield*: large meat market in Charterhouse Street. It opens at 4 a.m. It is located a few blocks north of St Bartholomew's Hospital, which, though not specified in the text, is the hospital in which Scene One takes place (the programme for the Cottesloe production featured photographs of Blackfriars, Smithfield, St Bartholomew's and Postman's Park).

9 *Postman's Park*: opened in 1880 on a former churchyard in Aldersgate, near Smithfield, the park was named after the General Post Office, which formed its southern boundary and was used by postmen in breaks between shifts. In 1887, the artist G.F. Watts wrote to *The Times* newspaper suggesting that Queen Victoria's Golden Jubilee be marked by a memorial honouring heroic acts by ordinary people in civilian life. In the absence of public support, Watts created a fifty-foot-long gallery himself, the Watts Memorial of Heroic Deeds, made from glazed Doulton china tablets, and opened in 1900. The Minotaur sculpture by Michael Ayrton, mentioned by Alice, was in the park when Marber wrote the play, but was removed a few years later because it was deemed pagan by the church who owned the land.

Borough: an area of London south of the Thames, which encompasses Ayres Street, named after the real Alice Ayres. It runs off Union Street, location of the fire in which she died.

Minotaur: mythical monster, half man, half bull.

16 *urban legend*: a story about the city that, over a long period of time, gains universal credence, even though

the incident may never actually have taken place. For instance, pet baby alligators were said to have been flushed down the lavatories in New York when they were no longer wanted and to have grown enormous in the sewers.

22 *steal his soul*: photography was thought by primitive people to steal the soul of the subject.

25 *Newton's Cradle*: extremely popular as a stress-relieving 'executive toy' in the 1980s. Five steel balls are suspended by thin wire from a rectangular metal frame, about 15 cm high. If you pull one ball back and release it the energy is transmitted through the three static balls and the last ball swings out then back again. If you pull two balls back and release them then the last two balls swing out, and so on. In physics, the cradle is used as a perfect demonstration of one of Sir Isaac Newton's 'Laws of Motion': the law of conservation of energy and momentum; in *Closer*, it is a metaphor for the physical and emotional knock-on effects of Dan and Alice's first encounter.

28 *perineum*: the highly sensitive section of flesh between the anus and the scrotum or vulva.

41 *seeing my first private patient*: on qualifying, all British doctors are obliged initially to work for the National Health Service, whose patients, broadly speaking, do not pay for their treatment. Doctors may subsequently opt to increase their earnings substantially by going partially or wholly into private practice, where patients pay. 'Going private' should be against Larry's professed socialist principles.

42 *Is he a fan of Man Ray or Karsh?*: Man Ray (1890–1977), American-born artist and photographer and co-founder of the Surrealist movement. Yousuf Karsh (1908–2002), Canadian photographer, known as 'Karsh of Ottawa' and celebrated for his black-and-white portraits of the famous and the powerful. Dan is mocking Larry's likely ignorance of both photographers and their work.

43 *Only because you* stalked *me outside my studio*: Anna is using the term jokingly, but when *Closer* opened, 'stalking'

and 'stalker' had recently come into common usage as labels for individuals, usually men, who obsessively pursued the objects of their unrequited affections, often celebrities. A number of high-profile prosecutions led to the introduction of 'anti-stalker' legislation.

46 *Cupid*: the god of love, responsible for bringing Larry and Anna together.

49 *Messerschmitt*: German bomber during the Second World War.

60 *First he went down on me and then we fucked*: 'to go down on' denotes oral sex, in this instance Dan performing cunnilingus on Anna.

66 *I'm in the skin trade*: Larry is punning on the common slang usage of the term 'skin trade' to denote prostitution, by applying it to his real profession as a dermatologist: a doctor specialising in diseases of the skin.

68 *A recent patient of 'Doctor Tit'*: Larry has noticed that one of Alice's lapdancing club colleagues has, like so many other strippers, had silicone breast implants.

69 *pneumatic robots*: another reference to the silicone-enhanced, gravity-defying artificiality of many lapdancers' bodies.
coked-up: high on cocaine.

99 *He is reading a Gideon's Bible*: founded in 1899 and based in Nashville, Tennessee, the Gideon's International Organisation distributes millions of Bibles in 181 countries in 82 languages, many of them placed in the bedside-table drawers of hotel and motel bedrooms.

113 *Forty-third and Madison*: Alice has been knocked down at the junction of Forty-third Street and Madison Avenue in mid-town Manhattan, New York City.

Questions for Further Study

1 'Anna is the heart of the play, Alice is the soul, Dan's the brains and Larry's the balls' (Patrick Marber). How appropriate are these shorthand descriptions of the characters and why do you think Marber chose them?

2 In Steven Soderbergh's film *sex, lies and videotape*, Graham tells Anne 'that men learn to love the person they're attracted to, and that women become more and more attracted to the person that they love'. To what extent do Anna, Alice, Dan and Larry confirm or contradict this notion?

3 'On some level, I believe that there is no such thing as an honest relationship. The best you can hope for is an honest relationship with yourself' (Patrick Marber in the *Sunday Times* Culture section, 1997). How useful is this comment in explaining the characters' attitudes towards truth and deceit in *Closer*?

4 *Closer* brings together a stripper, an obituarist, a photographer and a dermatologist. How do these professions reflect the play's exploration of human bodies, identity and mortality?

5 'Knifingly explicit, *Closer* is further proof that the addictive shortcuts of pornography have entered not only the cultural mainstream, but the bloodstream as well' (James Wolcott in *Vanity Fair*, March 1999). Do you consider *Closer* to be merely pornographic or does it have something true to say about human nature and society in 1990s Britain?

6 'For me, *Closer* was about the fact that the self who falls in and out of love may be a very different person from the one who walks the dog, goes to work and makes the tea' (Patrick Marber in the *Guardian*, January 1998). What does *Closer* reveal about the nature of identity, and the notion of a divided, ever-changing self?

7 'It is a mighty force that of mere chance, absolutely irresistible yet manifesting itself often in delicate forms such, for instance, as the charm, true or illusory, of a human being' (Joseph Conrad, *Chance*, 1914, quoted in the programme for the National Theatre premiere of *Closer*). What role do the 'delicate forms' of chance play in the lives of the characters in *Closer*? Is the use of chance convincing? Does it need to be?

8 'Alice is both shockingly confident and insecure simultaneously' (Patrick Marber). How does Marber illustrate these two contradictory aspects of Alice's character, and how do Dan and Larry respond to them?

9 The British posters for the film of *Closer* used this tagline: 'If you believe in love at first sight you never stop looking.' How accurately does this statement reflect the characters' contrasting attitudes to love and sex?

10 How do the London setting and the specific scene locations reflect or underline the themes of the play?

11 'Larry seems to be the most centred of the characters, but changes as he deals with all kinds of class, money and status anxieties' (Patrick Marber). Discuss the role played by class in *Closer*, with particular reference to the Anna–Larry relationship.

12 'One of the things that's happening in the play is the characters' increasing consciousness of their own mortality' (Patrick Marber). How does each character in *Closer* view ageing and mortality, and how does the prospect of death influence their actions?

13 A stage production of *Closer* allows more detachment and artificiality than a film. Do the gains of the film offset its losses?

14 'Yet each man kills the thing he loves' (Oscar Wilde, 'The Ballad of Reading Gaol', 1898). How useful is Wilde's line in understanding Larry's and Dan's behaviour in *Closer*?

15 'There *is* happiness in this play, and I found that the most difficult part of directing it was to make the scenes where the characters are in love un-squelchy and unsickening' (Patrick Marber, National Theatre

Platform, June 1997). Where and when are the characters in *Closer* genuinely happy, and how effectively does Marber contrast these moments with scenes of anger and recrimination?

16 Larry: 'Time: what a tricky little fucker' (*Closer*, Scene Six). How does the structure of *Closer* highlight the 'tricky' nature of time and its effect on our experience and recollection of intimate relationships?

17 Alice tells Larry: 'I'm not a whore' (p. 66); Larry says to Anna: 'Be my whore and in return I will pay you with your liberty' (p. 76). Using prostitution as a recurrent motif, how and why does Marber link money and sex in *Closer*?

18 'We all have a hunger for the truth. The characters are addicted to the truth, but no more than they're addicted to nicotine or love' (Patrick Marber, National Theatre Platform, June 1997). Choose three key moments from the play when a character lies or demands the truth from their current or ex-partner, and suggest why they do so.

19 Four characters, four couples, twelve scenes, spread across four years: how does the formal symmetry of *Closer* contribute to our understanding of the characters and the repetitive cycle of their experiences?

20 At the end of the film of *Closer*, Alice is alive and well and Anna and Larry are still living together. How far do these two facts alter our perception of the choices the characters make, compared to their fates in the play?

21 Compare and contrast the presentation of heterosexual desire in *Closer* with one or more of the following plays and films: Patrick Marber's *After Miss Julie*, Steven Soderbergh's *sex, lies and videotape*, David Mamet's *Sexual Perversity in Chicago*, Neil LaBute's *Your Friends & Neighbors*, Mike Nichols's *Carnal Knowledge*.

DANIEL ROSENTHAL was born in London in 1971 and educated at University College School, London, and Pembroke College, Cambridge. He has written on theatre and film for *The Times*, *Independent*, *Observer* and *Independent on Sunday*. He was Editor of the annual *Variety International Film Guide* 2002–6 and is the author of *Shakespeare on Screen* (2000) and *100 Shakespeare Films* (2007). He wrote the Commentary and Notes for the Methuen Student Edition of David Mamet's *Oleanna* and he is writing a major new history of the Royal National Theatre.

Methuen Drama World Classics

include

Jean Anouilh (two volumes)
Brendan Behan
Aphra Behn
Bertolt Brecht (eight volumes)
Büchner
Bulgakov
Calderón
Čapek
Anton Chekhov
Noël Coward (eight volumes)
Feydeau (two volumes)
Eduardo De Filippo
Max Frisch
John Galsworthy
Gogol
Gorky (two volumes)
Harley Granville Barker
  (two volumes)
Victor Hugo
Henrik Ibsen (six volumes)
Jarry

Lorca (three volumes)
Marivaux
Mustapha Matura
David Mercer (two volumes)
Arthur Miller (six volumes)
Molière
Musset
Peter Nichols (two volumes)
Joe Orton
A. W. Pinero
Luigi Pirandello
Terence Rattigan
  (two volumes)
W. Somerset Maugham
  (two volumes)
August Strindberg
  (three volumes)
J. M. Synge
Ramón del Valle-Inclán
Frank Wedekind
Oscar Wilde

Methuen Drama Student Editions

Jean Anouilh *Antigone* • John Arden *Serjeant Musgrave's Dance*
Alan Ayckbourn *Confusions* • Aphra Behn *The Rover* • Edward Bond
Lear • *Saved* • Bertolt Brecht *The Caucasian Chalk Circle* • *Fear and
Misery in the Third Reich* • *The Good Person of Szechwan* • *Life of Galileo* •
Mother Courage and her Children • *The Resistible Rise of Arturo Ui* • *The
Threepenny Opera* • Anton Chekhov *The Cherry Orchard* • *The Seagull* •
Three Sisters • *Uncle Vanya* • Caryl Churchill *Serious Money* • *Top Girls*
• Shelagh Delaney *A Taste of Honey* • Euripides *Elektra* • *Medea* •
Dario Fo *Accidental Death of an Anarchist* • Michael Frayn *Copenhagen*
• John Galsworthy *Strife* • Nikolai Gogol *The Government Inspector* •
Robert Holman *Across Oka* • Henrik Ibsen *A Doll's House* • *Ghosts* •
Hedda Gabler • Charlotte Keatley *My Mother Said I Never Should* •
Bernard Kops *Dreams of Anne Frank* • Federico García Lorca *Blood
Wedding* • *Doña Rosita the Spinster* (bilingual edition) • *The House of
Bernarda Alba* • (bilingual edition) • *Yerma* (bilingual edition) • David
Mamet *Glengarry Glen Ross* • *Oleanna* • Patrick Marber *Closer* • John
Marston *Malcontent* • Martin McDonagh *The Lieutenant of Inishmore* •
Joe Orton *Loot* • Luigi Pirandello *Six Characters in Search of an Author*
• Mark Ravenhill *Shopping and F***ing* • Willy Russell *Blood Brothers*
• *Educating Rita* • Sophocles *Antigone* • *Oedipus the King* • Wole
Soyinka *Death and the King's Horseman* • Shelagh Stephenson *The
Memory of Water* • August Strindberg *Miss Julie* • J. M. Synge *The
Playboy of the Western World* • Theatre Workshop *Oh What a Lovely
War* Timberlake Wertenbaker *Our Country's Good* • Arnold Wesker
The Merchant • Oscar Wilde *The Importance of Being Earnest* •
Tennessee Williams *A Streetcar Named Desire* • *The Glass Menagerie*

For a complete catalogue of Methuen Drama titles
write to:

Methuen Drama
Bloomsbury Publishing Plc
50 Bedford Square
London
WC1B 3DP

or you can visit our website at:

www.methuendrama.com